Positive Affirmations For Black Men

Rewire Your Brain For Success in 30 Days with Inspiring and Motivation Affirmations About Money, Wealth, Health, Confidence and Abundance

Daberechi N

Contents

Introduction

In this book, you will discover how to tap into the incredible power of affirmations to transform your life. Affirmations are a simple yet powerful tool that can help you change your thoughts, beliefs, and ultimately your life. Through this book, you will learn how to harness this power to create the life you truly desire.

You will be guided through the process of creating affirmations that are specific to your goals and desires, and learn how to use them effectively in your day-to-day life. This book is filled with practical strategies and exercises that you can start implementing right away to see real, tangible results.

By using affirmations, you will be able to shift your mindset, overcome limiting beliefs, and create a more positive and abundant life. You will learn how to use affirmations to attract more success, abundance, love, and happiness into your life.

With this book, you will gain a deeper understanding of the incredible power of affirmations and how to use them to create the life you truly desire. You will discover the transformational impact of positive self-talk and learn how to use it to your advantage.

Get ready to unlock your full potential and achieve your dreams with the help of this powerful guide. Your affirmation journey starts now.

Introduction

How To Use This Book

• Set your intention: Before beginning the affirmations, take a moment to reflect on what you hope to gain from this practice. What areas of your life do you want to improve? What kind of person do you want to be? Clarifying your intentions will give you a sense of direction as you work through the affirmations.

• Pick an affirmation: Each section of the book is focused on a different topic, such as health, wealth, love, or happiness. Choose a section that speaks to you and select an affirmation that resonates. You can also choose an affirmation at random or based on a particular situation or challenge you are facing.

• Repeat the affirmation: Say the affirmation out loud or in your head several times a day, preferably in the morning and before bed. Visualize the affirmation as if it is already true. Allow yourself to feel the emotions associated with the affirmation.

• Take action: Affirmations are most effective when combined with action. Take steps towards your goal, even if they are small. Your actions will help reinforce your belief in the affirmation and make it more likely to come true.

• Track your progress: Keep track of your progress and celebrate your successes. Look for evidence that the affirmation is coming true and acknowledge any changes you have noticed in yourself or your life.

• By following these steps, you will be able to use this book of affirmations to create positive change in your life and achieve your goals.

1. 100 Powerful Positive Affirmations For Wealth

1 I am worthy of financial abundance and success.

2 I am capable of creating wealth and achieving financial freedom.

3 I am smart, resourceful, and know how to make sound financial decisions.

4 I attract wealth and prosperity into my life every day.

5 My wealth and success inspire and uplift others in my community.

6 My wealth is a reflection of my hard work, persistence, and determination.

7 I have a positive relationship with money and view it as a tool for creating opportunities and freedom.

8 I am grateful for my current financial situation and remain open to receiving even more abundance in the future.

9 I am constantly expanding my wealth and learning new ways to generate income and create value.

10 I am financially savvy and make informed decisions that benefit me and those around me.

11 My wealth allows me to provide for my family and loved ones, creating a legacy of generational wealth.

12 I am an entrepreneur who creates value and solutions for my community, leading to financial success.

13 I am financially independent and free to pursue my passions and goals without fear or limitation.

14 My wealth allows me to give back to my community and make a positive impact on those around me.

15 I am financially literate and understand how to grow and manage my wealth effectively.

16 My mindset is aligned with wealth creation and abundance, leading to limitless possibilities and opportunities.

17 My financial success is a reflection of my self-worth and belief in my abilities.

18 I am open to new ideas and opportunities for wealth creation and financial growth.

19 I am a magnet for wealth, attracting abundance and prosperity effortlessly and naturally.

20 My wealth and success do not define me, but they do provide me with the freedom and flexibility to live life on my own terms.

21 I am committed to creating a legacy of wealth and financial empowerment for myself and future generations.

22 I am capable of creating multiple streams of income and diversifying my financial portfolio.

23 My wealth allows me to travel, explore, and experience the world in new and exciting ways.

24 I am confident in my abilities and talents, which enables me to create value and generate income in various ways.

25 My financial success does not come at the expense of others, but rather benefits and supports those around me.

26 I am patient and consistent in my pursuit of financial freedom and abundance, trusting that my hard work and dedication will pay off.

27 I am open to receiving financial blessings and opportunities from unexpected sources.

28 My wealth allows me to invest in myself, my personal growth, and my development as a leader and entrepreneur.

29 I am a positive influence on those around me, encouraging and inspiring them to pursue their own financial goals and dreams.

30 I am a master of my finances, able to make strategic and calculated decisions that lead to greater wealth and success.

31 My wealth and success do not diminish my humility, but rather enhance it, allowing me to remain grounded and grateful for my blessings.

32 I am constantly learning and growing, seeking out new information and strategies for wealth creation and management.

33 My financial success is a result of my discipline, focus, and unwavering commitment to my goals.

34 My wealth is a tool for creating positive change in the world and helping those who are less fortunate.

35 I am free from limiting beliefs and self-doubt, knowing that I am capable of achieving great financial success and abundance.

36 My financial success is a product of my positive mindset and alignment with the energy of wealth and abundance.

37 I am able to turn my passions and interests into profitable ventures that contribute to my lifestyle.

38 My financial success is a result of my ability to take calculated risks and make strategic investments.

39 I have a healthy relationship with money, viewing it as a tool for creating the life I desire.

40 I am surrounded by supportive and encouraging people who believe in my financial success and uplift me along the way.

41 My wealth allows me to create a comfortable and secure future for myself and my family.

42 I am deserving of financial abundance and success, regardless of any external factors.

43 I am a valuable asset to any organization, able to generate revenue and create value for my clients and customers.

44 My financial success is a result of my unwavering commitment to my goals, even in the face of challenges and setbacks.

45 I am constantly learning and growing, improving my financial literacy and expanding my financial knowledge.

46 I am able to maintain a healthy work-life balance, prioritizing my well-being and happiness while still achieving financial success.

47 My financial success is a result of my ability to leverage my skills and talents to create value in the marketplace.

48 I am able to create a positive impact on the world through my wealth and success, leaving a lasting legacy of change and progress.

49 I am able to give generously to those in need, using my financial resources to create a better world for everyone.

50 My wealth allows me to pursue my passions and live a life of purpose and fulfillment.

51 I am capable of achieving financial success in any industry or field, regardless of any perceived barriers or limitations.

52 My wealth is a result of my hard work, dedication, and persistence over time.

53 I am able to maintain a positive attitude and mindset, even in the face of financial challenges and adversity.

54 My financial success is a result of my ability to make smart, informed decisions that benefit myself and others.

55 I am able to create a diverse and resilient financial portfolio, minimizing risk and maximizing potential returns.

56 My wealth is a reflection of my commitment to creating value and solving problems for others.

57 I am able to create financial freedom and flexibility for myself and my loved ones, allowing us to live life on our own terms.

58 My financial success is a result of my ability to build and maintain strong relationships with my clients, customers, and partners.

59 I am able to overcome any financial obstacle or challenge with determination and persistence.

60 My wealth is a tool for creating positive change and progress in my community and the world at large.

Positive Affirmations For Black Men

61 I am capable of creating and sustaining multiple successful businesses and ventures.

62 My financial success is a product of my ability to think creatively and innovatively, constantly seeking out new opportunities and solutions.

63 I am able to manage and grow my wealth effectively, making wise financial decisions that benefit myself and those around me.

64 My wealth allows me to experience a comfortable and luxurious lifestyle, enjoying the fruits of my labor.

65 I am able to create a sense of financial security and stability for myself and my loved ones, reducing stress and anxiety.

66 My financial success is a result of my ability to take action and make things happen, rather than waiting for opportunities to come to me.

67 I am able to balance my financial goals and desires with my values and principles, remaining true to myself and my beliefs.

68 My wealth allows me to travel and explore the world, experiencing new cultures and adventures.

69 I am capable of building and leading successful teams and organizations, creating value and achieving financial success together.

70 My financial success is a result of my ability to adapt and evolve with the changing marketplace and economy.

71 I am able to create a positive impact on the environment and society through my financial resources and investments.

72 My financial success is a product of my willingness to learn from my mistakes and failures, using them as opportunities for growth and improvement.

73 I am able to inspire and motivate others to achieve their own financial success and create positive change in their own lives.

74 My wealth allows me to give back to my community and support causes that are important to me.

75 I am capable of creating and sustaining a legacy of wealth and success for future generations.

76 My financial success is a result of my ability to build and maintain a strong and supportive network of mentors, advisors, and peers.

77 I am able to create and maintain healthy financial habits, including budgeting, saving, and investing.

78 My wealth allows me to take care of myself and my loved ones, providing access to quality healthcare, education, and resources.

79 I am capable of achieving financial success without sacrificing my values or integrity.

80 My financial success is a result of my ability to persevere through challenges and setbacks, remaining focused on my goals.

81 I am able to enjoy my financial success without guilt or shame, embracing the abundance and opportunities it provides.

82 My wealth allows me to support and empower other black men in achieving their own financial goals and dreams.

83 I am capable of creating and implementing effective financial strategies that benefit myself and those around me.

84 My financial success is a product of my ability to identify and capitalize on emerging trends and opportunities in the marketplace.

85 I am able to create a sense of financial freedom and independence, allowing me to make choices based on my desires and passions rather than financial limitations.

86 My wealth allows me to pursue higher education and professional development, expanding my knowledge and skills.

87 I am capable of creating a healthy work-life balance that supports my financial goals and overall well-being.

88 My financial success is a result of my ability to think and act strategically, constantly seeking out new opportunities and solutions.

89 I am able to use my wealth to create positive change in my industry and in society as a whole.

90 My financial success is a product of my ability to remain disciplined and focused on my goals, even in the face of distractions and challenges.

91 I am capable of overcoming any financial challenge or obstacle with creativity and determination.

92 My wealth allows me to support and uplift other marginalized communities and individuals, creating a more just and equitable society.

93 I am able to create and maintain healthy and productive financial relationships with my business partners and investors.

94 My financial success is a result of my ability to identify and leverage my unique strengths and talents.

95 I am able to make wise and informed financial decisions, based on research and analysis rather than emotion or impulse.

96 My wealth allows me to live a life of purpose and fulfillment, pursuing my passions and making a positive impact in the world.

97 I am capable of creating a diverse and resilient financial portfolio that adapts to changing market conditions.

98 My financial success is a product of my ability to stay informed and up-to-date on financial trends and strategies.

99 My wealth allows me to create a sense of impact and influence in the world, using my resources to create positive change and make a difference in the lives of others, and it brings me a sense of purpose and fulfillment.

100 I am able to maintain a positive and abundant mindset, attracting wealth and success into my life.

2. 101 More Powerful Positive Affirmations For Wealth

1 My wealth allows me to create a life of abundance and prosperity for myself and those around me, while also creating a positive impact on the world.

2 Deeper Pyschological changes, Affirmations Including feelings and emotions

3 I deserve wealth and abundance in my life, and I feel grateful for the financial opportunities that come my way.

4 I feel confident in my ability to create and maintain a successful financial portfolio.

5 I am worthy of financial success and freedom, and I feel empowered to pursue my goals.

6 My financial abundance brings me a sense of security and peace of mind.

7 I am capable of achieving my financial dreams, and I feel motivated to take action towards my goals.

8 I am grateful for the financial education and resources that allow me to make informed decisions about my wealth.

9 I feel proud of my financial achievements and the positive impact they have on my life and community.

10 My wealth allows me to support and uplift other black men in achieving their own financial goals.

Positive Affirmations For Black Men

11 I am capable of creating a legacy of financial success and empowerment for future generations, and it brings me a sense of purpose and fulfillment.

12 My financial success allows me to live a life of abundance, joy, and freedom, and I feel grateful for the opportunities it provides.

13 I feel worthy and deserving of the abundance and financial success that comes my way.

14 My financial success brings me a sense of satisfaction and pride, and I feel motivated to continue to grow and expand my wealth.

15 I am capable of creating and implementing effective financial strategies that benefit myself and those around me, and it brings me a sense of confidence and empowerment.

16 My wealth allows me to take care of myself and my loved ones, providing a sense of security and comfort.

17 I am grateful for the financial opportunities and resources that allow me to make wise and informed decisions about my wealth.

18 I feel proud of my financial accomplishments, and it brings me a sense of fulfillment and purpose.

19 My financial success allows me to pursue my passions and make a positive impact in the world, and it brings me a sense of joy and satisfaction.

20 I am capable of overcoming any financial challenge or obstacle with creativity and determination, and it brings me a sense of resilience and strength.

21 My wealth allows me to live a life of freedom and independence, pursuing my desires and passions without financial limitations, and it brings me a sense of joy and fulfillment.

22 I feel confident in my ability to create and sustain a diverse and resilient financial portfolio, and it brings me a sense of security and stability.

23 I am grateful for the financial opportunities that come my way, and it brings me a sense of appreciation and contentment.

24 My financial success allows me to give back to my community and support causes that are important to me, and it brings me a sense of purpose and fulfillment.

25 I am capable of inspiring and motivating others to achieve their own financial success and create positive change in their own lives, and it brings me a sense of empowerment and pride.

26 My wealth allows me to pursue higher education and professional development, expanding my knowledge and skills, and it brings me a sense of growth and accomplishment.

27 I feel proud of my financial accomplishments, and it brings me a sense of confidence and self-worth.

28 My financial success is a result of my ability to think and act strategically, constantly seeking out new opportunities and solutions, and it brings me a sense of creativity and ingenuity.

29 I am capable of creating a sense of financial freedom and independence, allowing me to make choices based on my desires and passions rather than financial limitations, and it brings me a sense of joy and fulfillment.

30 My wealth allows me to create positive change in my industry and in society as a whole, and it brings me a sense of purpose and impact.

31 I feel confident in my ability to create and maintain healthy financial habits, including budget of my financial resources, and it brings me a sense of discipline and responsibility.

32 30. I am grateful for the financial mentors and role models who have inspired and guided me along my path to financial success, and it brings me a sense of appreciation and gratitude.

33 My financial success allows me to create a sense of security and stability for myself and those around me, and it brings me a sense of peace and comfort.

34 I am capable of adapting to changes in the financial landscape and creating new opportunities for growth and success, and it brings me a sense of flexibility and adaptability.

35 My wealth allows me to invest in myself and my personal growth, including my physical, emotional, and spiritual wellbeing, and it brings me a sense of self-care and self-love.

36 I feel proud of the financial legacy I am creating for myself and my family, and it brings me a sense of generational impact and empowerment.

37 I am grateful for the financial experiences, both positive and negative, that have shaped me and taught me valuable lessons, and it brings me a sense of wisdom and insight.

38 My financial success allows me to take risks and pursue opportunities that may have seemed out of reach before, and it brings me a sense of adventure and excitement.

39 I am capable of creating financial abundance and success without sacrificing my integrity and values, and it brings me a sense of authenticity and alignment.

40 My wealth allows me to support and uplift other black men in their pursuit of financial success, and it brings me a sense of community and connection.

41 I feel confident in my ability to make wise and informed decisions about my wealth, and it brings me a sense of clarity and certainty.

42 My financial success allows me to create a sense of freedom and independence, allowing me to make choices based on my desires and passions rather than financial limitations, and it brings me a sense of joy and fulfillment.

43 I am grateful for the financial blessings that come my way, and it brings me a sense of abundance and prosperity.

44 My financial success allows me to create a positive impact on the world, contributing to important causes and making a difference in the lives of others, and it brings me a sense of purpose and meaning.

45 I am capable of manifesting my financial dreams and desires through focused intention and action, and it brings me a sense of empowerment and self-belief.

46 My wealth allows me to invest in my future, both financially and personally, and it brings me a sense of hope and optimism.

47 I feel proud of the financial accomplishments that I have achieved, and it brings me a sense of confidence and self-esteem.

48 My financial success is a result of my hard work, dedication, and perseverance, and it brings me a sense of achievement and satisfaction.

49 I am capable of creating a diverse and resilient financial portfolio that withstands the ups and downs of the economy, and it brings me a sense of security and stability.

50 My wealth allows me to pursue my passions and live life on my own terms, and it brings me a sense of freedom and fulfillment.

51 I feel grateful for the financial support and opportunities that have helped me to achieve my goals, and it brings me a sense of humility and appreciation.

52 My financial success allows me to create a positive legacy for myself and future generations, and it brings me a sense of pride and legacy.

53 I am capable of using my financial resources to make a positive difference in my community, and it brings me a sense of contribution and impact.

54 My wealth allows me to create a sense of security and stability for my family and loved ones, and it brings me a sense of peace and comfort.

55 I feel proud of the financial mindset that I have cultivated, allowing me to make wise and informed decisions about my finances, and it brings me a sense of confidence and self-assuredness.

56 54. My financial success allows me to create a sense of balance and harmony in my life, allowing me to focus on other areas of my personal growth, and it brings me a sense of holistic wellbeing.

57 I am capable of overcoming financial setbacks and obstacles with resilience and determination, and it brings me a sense of strength and perseverance.

58 My wealth allows me to take care of myself and those around me, allowing me to live a life of abundance and generosity, and it brings me a sense of fulfillment and joy.

59 I feel grateful for the financial education and resources that have empowered me to create my own financial success, and it brings me a sense of appreciation and gratitude.

60 My financial success allows me to pursue my dreams and goals, whether personal or professional, and it brings me a sense of accomplishment and fulfillment.

61 I am capable of creating financial abundance through hard work, dedication, and smart decision-making, and it brings me a sense of pride and self-belief.

62 My wealth allows me to give back to my community, supporting important causes and initiatives, and it brings me a sense of purpose and impact.

63 I feel proud of the financial habits and practices that I have developed, allowing me to create a sustainable and fulfilling financial life, and it brings me a sense of self-worth and self-respect.

Positive Affirmations For Black Men

64 My financial success allows me to travel and explore the world, opening up new experiences and opportunities, and it brings me a sense of adventure and discovery.

65 I am capable of creating a legacy of financial knowledge and empowerment, sharing my experiences and insights with others to help them achieve their own financial success, and it brings me a sense of mentorship and leadership.

66 My wealth allows me to take care of my loved ones, providing for them and creating a sense of security, and it brings me a sense of love and responsibility.

67 I feel grateful for the financial resources and opportunities that have come my way, and it brings me a sense of humility and appreciation.

68 My financial success allows me to create a sense of stability and safety in my life, and it brings me a sense of peace and tranquility.

69 I am capable of creating financial abundance without sacrificing my personal values and beliefs, and it brings me a sense of authenticity and alignment.

70 My wealth allows me to invest in my own personal development and growth, learning new skills and pursuing my passions, and it brings me a sense of curiosity and exploration.

71 I feel proud of the financial decisions that I have made, knowing that they have led me to a life of abundance and success, and it brings me a sense of confidence and self-esteem.

72 My financial success allows me to create a sense of freedom and flexibility in my life, allowing me to make choices based on my desires and aspirations, and it brings me a sense of joy and fulfillment.

73 I am capable of managing my financial resources with wisdom and prudence, creating a sustainable and long-term financial plan, and it brings me a sense of responsibility and maturity.

74 My wealth allows me to support my community and create positive change in the world, and it brings me a sense of contribution and impact.

75 I feel proud of the financial goals that I have achieved, knowing that they have required hard work, dedication, and persistence, and it brings me a sense of accomplishment and satisfaction.

76 My financial success allows me to create a sense of security and safety for my family and loved ones, and it brings me a sense of love and care.

77 I am capable of overcoming financial challenges and obstacles, using my skills, knowledge, and resources to find creative and effective solutions, and it brings me a sense of resilience and resourcefulness.

78 My wealth allows me to live a life of abundance and prosperity, enjoying the pleasures and luxuries that come with financial success, and it brings me a sense of enjoyment and satisfaction.

79 I feel grateful for the financial support and guidance that I have received from mentors and role models, and it brings me a sense of appreciation and respect.

80 My financial success allows me to create a legacy of financial empowerment for future generations, and it brings me a sense of purpose and impact.

81 I am capable of achieving financial success without compromising my integrity or values, and it brings me a sense of authenticity and alignment.

82 My wealth allows me to invest in my own health and wellbeing, taking care of my physical, mental, and emotional needs, and it brings me a sense of vitality and energy.

83 I feel proud of the financial independence and freedom that I have achieved, knowing that I have the power to make my own choices and decisions, and it brings me a sense of autonomy and self-determination.

84 My financial success allows me to support and contribute to important social and environmental causes, and it brings me a sense of social responsibility and impact.

85 I am capable of creating financial abundance through hard work, discipline, and a positive mindset, and it brings me a sense of motivation and inspiration.

86 My wealth allows me to create opportunities and support for those who are less fortunate, and it brings me a sense of generosity and kindness.

87 I feel grateful for the financial freedom and flexibility that I have created in my life, allowing me to pursue my passions and goals, and it brings me a sense of creativity and innovation.

88 My financial success allows me to create a sense of stability and security for my future, and it brings me a sense of peace of mind and comfort.

89 I am capable of overcoming financial setbacks and challenges, using my resilience and adaptability to find solutions and opportunities, and it brings me a sense of strength and courage.

Positive Affirmations For Black Men

90 My wealth allows me to create a legacy of financial knowledge and empowerment for my community, and it brings me a sense of leadership and influence.

91 I feel proud of the financial achievements and successes that I have accomplished, and it brings me a sense of accomplishment and fulfillment.

92 My financial success allows me to create a sense of purpose and meaning in my life, using my resources to support causes and initiatives that align with my values and beliefs, and it brings me a sense of passion and purpose.

93 I am capable of managing my financial resources with discipline and intention, creating a sustainable and responsible financial plan, and it brings me a sense of self-mastery and control.

94 My wealth allows me to create opportunities for myself and those around me, whether it be through investing, entrepreneurship, or philanthropy, and it brings me a sense of opportunity and potential.

95 I feel grateful for the financial support and resources that I have received from my community and society, and it brings me a sense of gratitude and responsibility.

96 My financial success allows me to create a sense of abundance and prosperity in my life, and it brings me a sense of joy and gratitude.

97 I am capable of creating a life of financial abundance and success, using my skills, knowledge, and resources to create value and wealth, and it brings me a sense of empowerment and capability.

98 My wealth allows me to live a life of freedom and flexibility, allowing me to make choices and decisions based on my own desires and aspirations, and it brings me a sense of liberation and self-expression.

99 I feel proud of the financial education and knowledge that I have acquired

100 My financial success allows me to support my family and loved ones, providing them with financial stability and security, and it brings me a sense of love and gratitude.

101 I am capable of creating a life of financial abundance and success, regardless of the challenges and obstacles that may arise, using my determination and resilience to overcome any setbacks, and it brings me a sense of perseverance and determination.

3. 207 Powerful Positive Affirmations For Money

1 Money flows to me easily and effortlessly.

2 I am worthy of financial abundance and prosperity.

3 I am grateful for the financial abundance in my life.

4 I attract money and abundance with every thought I think.

5 I am in control of my finances and my financial future.

6 I make smart financial decisions that lead to success and wealth.

7 I am confident in my ability to make money and create wealth.

8 Money is a positive force in my life and brings me joy and happiness.

9 I am deserving of financial success and abundance.

10 I am grateful for the abundance of money and resources that flow into my life.

11 I am open to receiving all of the financial blessings that come my way.

12 I am capable of creating wealth and financial success in my life.

13 My financial success is a reflection of my hard work and dedication.

14 I trust myself to make wise financial decisions.

15 I have an abundance mindset that attracts wealth and success to me.

16 I am focused on creating a life of financial abundance and prosperity.

Positive Affirmations For Black Men

17 My financial success allows me to live the life of my dreams.

18 I am in alignment with the energy of wealth and abundance.

19 I am constantly improving my financial situation and creating more wealth.

20 I am worthy of having financial freedom and security.

21 Money comes to me easily and effortlessly in all areas of my life.

22 I am grateful for the financial opportunities that come my way.

23 I am capable of creating financial abundance no matter what my current circumstances are.

24 I have a positive relationship with money and it is always there for me when I need it.

25 I am worthy of receiving financial abundance and prosperity in all areas of my life.

26 I am open to receiving unexpected financial blessings.

27 I am confident in my ability to manage and grow my wealth.

28 Money is a tool that I use to create a life of happiness and fulfillment.

29 My financial success allows me to contribute to my community and make a positive impact in the world.

30 I am constantly learning and growing in my financial knowledge and skills.

31 I am grateful for the abundance of opportunities to create wealth and financial success.

32 I am always surrounded by people who support my financial success and growth.

33 I trust in the universe to provide me with all the financial resources I need.

34 I am grateful for the wealth and abundance that flows into my life every day.

35 I am capable of creating a life of financial abundance and prosperity for myself and my loved ones.

36 I am open to new and innovative ways of creating wealth and financial success.

37 My financial success allows me to live the life of my dreams and achieve my goals.

38 I am deserving of financial freedom and security.

39 I am always taking steps to improve my financial situation and create more wealth.

40 I am confident in my ability to make smart financial decisions and investments.

41 I am grateful for the financial blessings that come my way.

42 I am worthy of receiving financial abundance and prosperity.

43 Money is a positive force in my life and it brings me joy and happiness.

44 I am grateful for the abundance of financial opportunities that come my way.

45 I am capable of creating wealth and financial success no matter what my current circumstances are.

46 I am constantly taking action to improve my financial situation and create more wealth.

47 I am grateful for the abundance of financial resources that are available to me.

48 Money is a tool that I use to create a life of happiness, joy, and fulfillment.

49 I am always attracting new opportunities for financial success and abundance.

50 I trust myself to make smart financial decisions that lead to success and wealth.

51 I am always learning and growing in my financial knowledge and skills.

52 I am grateful for the wealth and abundance that flows into my life.

53 Money flows to me easily and effortlessly in all areas of my life.

54 I am constantly surrounded by people who support my financial success and growth.

55 I am capable of creating a life of financial abundance and prosperity no matter what my current circumstances are.

56 I am constantly taking steps to improve my financial situation and create more wealth.

57 Money is a tool that I use to create the life of my dreams.

58 I trust myself to make wise financial decisions that lead to success and wealth.

59 My financial success allows me to live a life of joy, fulfillment, and happiness.

Positive Affirmations For Black Men

60 I am capable of creating wealth and financial success through my talents and skills.

61 I am confident in my ability to make smart financial decisions that lead to success and wealth.

62 I am grateful for the wealth and abundance that flows into my life each and everyday with ease.

63 I am in control of my financial future and I create abundance every day.

64 I am deserving of wealth and abundance, and I receive it with gratitude.

65 My financial success allows me to live a life of purpose and make a positive impact in the world.

66 I trust in my ability to create wealth and financial success, and I take action every day to achieve it.

67 I am worthy of wealth and abundance.

68 I am grateful for the money that comes into my life.

69 I trust that I will always have the financial resources I need.

70 My financial success brings me joy and peace of mind.

71 I feel confident in my ability to make money and manage it wisely.

72 I release any negative beliefs I have about money and welcome abundance into my life.

73 My wealth allows me to support and uplift my community.

74 I am abundant in all areas of my life, including my finances.

75 I am open and receptive to new money-making opportunities.

76 I attract abundance with ease and grace.

77 I feel secure in my financial present and future.

78 My financial success empowers me to live the life of my dreams.

79 I trust that my financial goals will manifest in perfect timing.

80 My wealth enables me to be of service to others.

81 I am abundant and prosperous, and I feel it in every fiber of my being.

82 I am grateful for the financial lessons I have learned, and they serve me well.

83 My wealth allows me to create a legacy of abundance for future generations.

84 I am deserving of wealth and prosperity, and I claim it now.

85 I trust in my ability to make wise financial decisions.

86 I feel confident in my ability to overcome any financial challenges that come my way.

87 My wealth allows me to experience the joys of life without worry or stress.

88 I am grateful for the abundance that flows into my life in expected and unexpected ways.

89 I am at peace with my financial situation, and I trust that it will continue to improve.

90 I am worthy of financial abundance, and I allow it to flow into my life.

91 My financial success is a blessing that I cherish and appreciate.

92 I am grateful for the abundance that surrounds me every day.

93 I release any fears or doubts about money and welcome prosperity into my life.

94 I trust in my ability to make money and grow my wealth.

95 My financial success is a source of inspiration for others.

96 I am grateful for the financial abundance that allows me to give generously to others.

97 I am abundant and prosperous, and I feel it in every aspect of my life.

98 My wealth allows me to pursue my passions and live a fulfilling life.

99 I trust in my ability to create a life of financial freedom and abundance.

100 I am worthy of wealth and prosperity, and I claim it with confidence and gratitude.

101 My financial success is a result of my positive mindset and hard work.

102 I feel empowered by my financial success and use it to make positive changes in the world.

103 My wealth allows me to live a life of purpose and meaning.

104 I am grateful for the abundance that surrounds me, and I use it to create more good in the world.

Positive Affirmations For Black Men

105 I am worthy of abundance, and I welcome it into my life with open arms.

106 My financial success allows me to live the life of my dreams and inspire others to do the same.

107 I am grateful for the financial blessings that come into my life every day.

108 I release any limiting beliefs I have about money and welcome abundance into my life.

109 My wealth allows me to support and uplift my loved ones.

110 I am worthy of abundance and success.

111 My financial goals are achievable, and I am taking steps to make them a reality.

112 Money flows effortlessly into my life and I am grateful for it.

113 I am financially free and have the power to make choices that align with my goals and values.

114 The universe supports me in achieving my financial goals.

115 Every dollar I spend comes back to me multiplied.

116 I release any limiting beliefs I have about money and open myself up to abundance.

117 I have the power to manifest my financial dreams into reality.

118 Every day, I am moving closer to my financial goals.

119 I am capable of creating and maintaining wealth.

120 Wealth and success come naturally to me.

121 I am worthy of all the wealth and abundance the universe has to offer.

122 My financial abundance positively impacts the lives of those around me.

123 I am constantly attracting new opportunities for financial growth and success.

124 My financial prosperity continues to expand with ease and joy.

125 I am grateful for the abundance and prosperity that flows into my life.

126 I am worthy of a life of luxury and comfort.

127 I am in control of my financial destiny.

128 I am attracting wealth and abundance effortlessly and joyfully.

129 I trust that the universe has a plan for my financial success.

130 Money is a tool that allows me to live the life I desire.

131 I have a deep sense of gratitude for all the financial blessings in my life.

132 I am a magnet for financial abundance and success.

133 I am creating a life of abundance and financial freedom for myself and my loved ones.

134 My bank account is overflowing with abundance and prosperity.

135 I am attracting financial opportunities with every thought and action.

136 I am financially abundant, and my future is filled with possibilities.

137 I am worthy of the best that life has to offer, including financial abundance.

138 The universe is conspiring in my favor to help me achieve my financial goals.

139 I am grateful for the abundance of wealth and prosperity in my life.

140 I have an abundance mindset and am constantly attracting new financial opportunities.

141 My financial abundance is a reflection of my inner abundance.

142 I am deserving of all the financial success that comes my way.

143 I am confident in my ability to create and maintain wealth.

144 I am attracting wealth and abundance into my life every day.

145 I am open and receptive to new financial opportunities and possibilities.

146 I am grateful for the financial freedom that allows me to live the life I desire.

147 I am constantly expanding my financial intelligence and knowledge.

148 I am worthy of a life of financial ease and comfort.

149 Money comes to me in unexpected and wonderful ways.

150 I trust that my financial success is inevitable.

151 I am abundant in every aspect of my life, including my finances.

152 My financial success benefits not only myself but those around me as well.

Positive Affirmations For Black Men

153 I am creating a life of financial abundance and freedom for myself and future generations.

154 I am worthy of all the financial blessings the universe has to offer.

155 I am attracting abundance and wealth in all areas of my life.

156 I am grateful for the financial blessings that have come my way and those that are on their way.

157 My financial success is a reflection of my commitment to my goals and values.

158 I am grateful for the abundance of money and resources in my life.

159 I am worthy of wealth and success.

160 I am deserving of all the financial blessings coming my way.

161 I am excited to see the money flow effortlessly into my life.

162 I am surrounded by people who support my financial goals and dreams.

163 I am capable of creating unlimited wealth and abundance in my life.

164 I am open and receptive to all forms of financial prosperity.

165 I am confident in my ability to manage and grow my finances.

166 I am focused on achieving my financial goals and aspirations.

167 I am constantly learning and growing in my understanding of wealth and money.

168 I am blessed with a sharp and intuitive financial mind.

169 I am willing to take calculated risks to achieve my financial goals.

170 I am fearless in pursuing opportunities for financial growth and success.

171 I am always attracting new and exciting financial opportunities.

172 I am motivated and determined to create a life of financial freedom.

173 I am releasing all negative beliefs and emotions about money and wealth.

174 I am stepping into a new realm of financial abundance and prosperity.

175 I am living a life of wealth and abundance in all areas of my life.

176 I am creating a positive relationship with money and wealth.

177 I am grateful for the opportunity to live a life of financial freedom.

178 I am embracing a mindset of abundance and prosperity.

179 I am in complete control of my financial destiny.

180 I am attracting financial prosperity effortlessly and with ease.

181 I am seeing the manifestation of my financial dreams and goals.

182 I am surrounded by a positive and supportive financial environment.

183 I am achieving my financial goals with grace and ease.

184 I am blessed with the skills and abilities to achieve financial abundance.

185 I am worthy of all the financial blessings coming my way.

186 I am attracting an abundance of wealth and prosperity.

187 I am grateful for all the money and resources coming into my life.

188 I am excited to see my finances grow and flourish.

189 I am worthy of receiving wealth and financial success.

190 I am attracting financial success into my life with every thought and action.

191 I am grateful for the many blessings of abundance in my life.

192 I am capable of achieving any financial goal I set for myself.

193 I am open to receiving financial abundance from unexpected sources.

194 I am creating a future of financial stability and security.

195 I am grateful for the many opportunities to create wealth and financial success.

196 I am confident in my ability to create a financially secure future.

197 I am worthy of financial success and abundance.

198 I am attracting financial prosperity with my positive thoughts and emotions.

199 I am creating a life of financial freedom and abundance.

200 I am attracting an abundance of financial opportunities into my life.

201 I am worthy of receiving all the financial blessings coming my way.

202 I am grateful for the many blessings of wealth and abundance in my life.

Positive Affirmations For Black Men

203 I am attracting wealth and success into my life with every thought and action.

204 I am capable of achieving unlimited financial success and prosperity.

205 I am grateful for the financial freedom and abundance in my life.

206 I am worthy of all the financial blessings the universe has in store for me.

207 I am living a life of abundance and prosperity in all areas of my life.

4. 226 Powerful Positive Affirmations For Success

1 I am worthy of success in all areas of my life.

2 Success comes naturally to me.

3 I am deserving of the success I desire.

4 I attract success effortlessly.

5 I am confident in my ability to achieve success.

6 Success is my birthright.

7 I am grateful for all of the success that I have achieved.

8 I have a powerful vision for my success.

9 My success benefits not only me, but those around me.

10 I am fully committed to my success.

11 I embrace challenges as opportunities for growth and success.

12 I am capable of achieving anything I set my mind to.

13 I am worthy of the success and abundance I desire.

14 I am constantly achieving new levels of success.

15 I trust in my ability to manifest the success I desire.

16 Success is not just an outcome, but a way of life.

Positive Affirmations For Black Men

17 I am constantly attracting new opportunities for success.

18 My success inspires those around me to achieve their own.

19 I am confident in my ability to overcome any obstacle and achieve success.

20 My hard work and dedication will lead to great success.

21 I am open to receiving all forms of success and abundance.

22 I believe in my ability to create my own success.

23 Success is a journey, and I am enjoying every step of it.

24 I am constantly learning and growing, which leads to greater success.

25 I am grateful for the success I have achieved, and excited for what is to come.

26 I trust the universe to provide me with the success I desire.

27 Success is a reflection of my positive mindset and actions.

28 I am constantly moving closer to my goals and achieving success.

29 Success is not just about money or material possessions, but about living a fulfilling life.

30 I am in control of my own success, and I choose to succeed.

31 I am surrounded by positive energy and opportunities for success.

32 I am worthy of the success and abundance that is available to me.

33 My success empowers me to inspire others to succeed as well.

34 I am grateful for all of the challenges I have overcome on my path to success.

35 Success is not just about what I do, but who I am as a person.

36 I am constantly developing new skills and abilities to achieve greater success.

37 I am confident in my ability to create my own success and abundance.

38 I am worthy of achieving all of my wildest dreams and desires.

39 My success is a direct result of my positive mindset and actions.

40 I am open to receiving unexpected forms of success and abundance.

41 I trust in the universe to provide me with all of the resources I need to achieve success.

42 Success is not just about the end result, but the journey along the way.

43 I am constantly expanding my comfort zone to achieve greater success.

44 I am capable of achieving extraordinary levels of success.

45 I am always moving forward and making progress towards my goals.

46 My success is a reflection of my determination, perseverance, and hard work.

47 I trust in my ability to attract the people and opportunities I need to achieve success.

48 I am open to learning from my mistakes and using them as stepping stones towards success.

49 Success is not just about what I achieve, but the person I become in the process.

50 I am worthy of all of the success and abundance that is available to me.

51 My success is not limited by external circumstances, but by my own mindset and actions.

52 I am capable of achieving greatness in all aspects of my life.

53 My potential for success is limitless.

54 Success comes easily and naturally to me.

55 My mind is clear and focused on my goals.

56 I am constantly growing and improving myself.

57 I embrace challenges as opportunities for growth and learning.

58 I am worthy of all the success and abundance I desire.

59 I am the architect of my own success and happiness.

60 I am in control of my own destiny and my success is inevitable.

61 My success inspires and uplifts those around me.

62 I radiate confidence, poise, and success in everything I do.

63 I am grateful for every success and achievement, big or small.

64 I am a magnet for success, wealth, and abundance.

65 My success allows me to give back to my community and those in need.

66 I am committed to creating a legacy of success and impact.

Positive Affirmations For Black Men

67 I am resilient and determined in the face of any obstacle or setback.

68 My actions align with my values and propel me towards success.

69 My success empowers me to live a life of freedom and fulfillment.

70 I am constantly pushing my own limits and reaching new levels of success.

71 Success is my birthright and I claim it with gratitude and humility.

72 I celebrate the success and achievements of others as I know it is a reflection of what is possible for me too.

73 I am capable of accomplishing anything I set my mind to.

74 Every day, I am getting closer and closer to my goals and achieving my vision of success.

75 Success is a journey, and I am grateful for every step of the way.

76 My success benefits not only me, but also my family, community, and future generations.

77 I am worthy of respect, recognition, and admiration for my success and accomplishments.

78 I am driven, focused, and disciplined in my pursuit of success.

79 My success is built on a foundation of hard work, determination, and passion.

80 I am worthy of all the success and abundance that life has to offer.

81 My success is not determined by my circumstances, but by my mindset and actions.

82 I am open to new opportunities and possibilities that can lead to even greater success.

83 Every day, I am becoming a better version of myself and inching closer to my vision of success.

84 I am proud of my achievements and take ownership of my success.

85 My success is a testament to the power of resilience, dedication, and grit.

86 I choose to surround myself with supportive and uplifting individuals who contribute to my success.

87 I am grateful for the lessons and growth that come with every success and every failure.

88 I am a trailblazer and a role model for others who aspire to success.

89 I am worthy of success regardless of any external factors, such as race, ethnicity, or socio-economic status.

90 I trust in my ability to overcome any challenge and achieve any goal I set for myself.

91 My success is a reflection of my commitment to excellence and unwavering faith in myself.

92 I am always learning, growing, and expanding my knowledge and skills to elevate my success.

93 My success is not just for me, but for the betterment of society as a whole.

94 I am grateful for the many blessings and opportunities that contribute to my success.

95 My success is an ongoing journey, and I am committed to staying the course no matter what.

96 I am successful in everything I set out to accomplish.

97 I am grateful for the successes that I have achieved, and I celebrate each one.

98 Success is my natural state, and I attract it effortlessly.

99 I am confident in my ability to achieve my goals and create the life I desire.

100 I have the discipline and focus necessary to achieve anything I set my mind to.

101 I am capable of achieving greatness, and I am committed to doing so.

102 I am motivated and driven to succeed, and I take action towards my goals every day.

103 I am surrounded by positivity and success, and it fuels my own success.

104 I am constantly growing and improving, and success is a natural result of my efforts.

105 I am proud of my achievements and am always striving for even greater success.

106 Every challenge is an opportunity for me to grow and achieve even greater success.

Positive Affirmations For Black Men

107 I am grateful for the setbacks I have experienced because they have led me to greater success.

108 My success benefits not only myself but also those around me.

109 I am a leader in my field, and my success inspires others to achieve their own goals.

110 My success is not limited by external circumstances, but rather by my own mindset and actions.

111 I have the ability to create opportunities and success wherever I go.

112 I am worthy and deserving of all the success that comes my way.

113 I trust in my ability to overcome any obstacle and achieve my goals.

114 Success is a state of mind, and I choose to think positively and focus on my goals.

115 I am focused on my vision of success and take action every day to make it a reality.

116 My success is a reflection of my hard work, dedication, and commitment to my goals.

117 I am open to new opportunities and ideas that will lead to even greater success.

118 I believe in myself and my ability to create a successful and fulfilling life.

119 Success is not a destination but a journey, and I am enjoying every step of the way.

120 My positive attitude and mindset attract success and abundance into my life.

121 I am confident in my abilities and know that I can achieve anything I set my mind to.

122 I am surrounded by people who support and encourage my success.

123 My success is not limited by my past experiences, but rather by my willingness to take action towards my goals.

124 I am grateful for the lessons I have learned on my path to success, and I use them to grow even stronger.

125 Success is not just about achieving external accomplishments but also about inner growth and personal development.

126 I am constantly learning and growing, and this leads to greater success in all areas of my life.

127 I am worthy of all the success that comes my way, and I use it to benefit myself and others.

128 I am a magnet for success, and it comes to me effortlessly and abundantly.

129 I am capable of achieving even greater success than I have imagined for myself.

130 My success is a result of my own hard work, dedication, and perseverance.

131 I am proud of my accomplishments and am constantly pushing myself to achieve even more.

132 I am grateful for the opportunities that have led me to success, and I use them to create even more opportunities.

133 My success is not limited by external circumstances, but rather by my own beliefs and actions.

134 I am surrounded by people who inspire and motivate me to achieve my goals and reach new levels of success.

135 I am worthy of success and all that comes with it.

136 I believe in my ability to achieve greatness.

137 Success is my birthright and I claim it now.

138 Every day, I am moving closer and closer to my goals.

139 I trust in the journey towards success and enjoy the process.

140 My success is a reflection of my hard work and dedication.

141 I am capable of overcoming any obstacle in my path to success.

142 Every setback is an opportunity to learn and grow stronger.

143 I am surrounded by positive and supportive people who encourage my success.

144 My success inspires and uplifts others to reach for their dreams.

145 Success is not only possible for me, but inevitable.

146 My mind is aligned with the frequency of success, and I attract it effortlessly.

147 I am in control of my destiny and choose to create a successful life.

Positive Affirmations For Black Men

148 I am committed to the daily habits and actions that lead to success.

149 I am grateful for the opportunities that have led me to where I am now, and excited for what's to come.

150 I am focused and determined to achieve my goals, and nothing can stop me.

151 My success comes from my own unique talents and abilities.

152 I trust my intuition to guide me towards success.

153 I am capable of achieving success in all areas of my life.

154 I am worthy of the recognition and accolades that come with success.

155 My success is a testament to the strength and resilience of black men.

156 I choose to see challenges as opportunities for growth and success.

157 I have a clear vision of what success looks and feels like for me.

158 I celebrate my successes, no matter how small they may seem.

159 I am open to new opportunities and experiences that will lead me to success.

160 I am creating a legacy of success for future generations.

161 Success is not just about financial gain, but also about personal fulfillment and happiness.

162 I trust that the universe is conspiring in my favor to help me achieve success.

163 I am worthy of abundance and success in all areas of my life.

164 I am constantly learning and growing, which leads me to greater success.

165 I am committed to taking action towards my goals every day.

166 Success is not an overnight phenomenon, but a result of consistent effort over time.

167 I am deserving of success and all the good things that come with it.

168 I am grateful for the lessons and experiences that have prepared me for success.

169 My success inspires and uplifts my community.

170 I am attracting opportunities for success with ease and grace.

171 I am worthy of being in positions of power and leadership, and I use it to uplift and empower others.

172 My success is a reflection of my resilience and strength in the face of adversity.

173 I choose to focus on the positive aspects of my journey towards success.

174 I am surrounded by mentors and role models who inspire and guide me towards success.

175 I am constantly expanding my knowledge and skills to increase my chances of success.

176 I am grateful for the support and encouragement of my loved ones on my journey towards success.

177 Success is a mindset, and I choose to cultivate a mindset of abundance and prosperity.

178 I am worthy of recognition and respect for my achievements.

179 I am proud of who I am and where I come from, and use it as a driving force towards success.

180 I am worthy of achieving great success.

181 I am confident in my ability to achieve my goals.

182 I am constantly improving and growing towards success.

183 Success is my birthright and I claim it.

184 I am grateful for the opportunities that lead me to success.

185 I am determined to succeed no matter the challenges I face.

186 I believe in myself and my ability to achieve success.

187 I am attracting success into my life every day.

188 I am proud of the success that I have achieved so far.

189 I am grateful for the skills and talents that have led me to success.

190 I am open to new opportunities and possibilities for success.

191 I am worthy of achieving my dreams and goals.

192 I am committed to my own success and growth.

193 I am persistent in my pursuit of success.

194 I am capable of achieving even more than I imagine.

Positive Affirmations For Black Men

195 I am successful in everything that I do.

196 I am constantly learning and growing towards success.

197 I am deserving of all the success that comes my way.

198 I am grateful for the setbacks that have taught me valuable lessons on my path to success.

199 I am in control of my own success.

200 I am worthy of the recognition and rewards that come with success.

201 I am confident in my ability to overcome any obstacle on my path to success.

202 I am successful in my own unique way.

203 I am proud of the success of others and celebrate it with them.

204 I am attracting opportunities and people that will help me achieve my goals.

205 I am surrounded by positive energy that fuels my success.

206 I am capable of achieving even the most challenging of my goals.

207 I am constantly moving towards greater success and abundance.

208 I am grateful for all the blessings that have led me to success.

209 I am confident in my ability to create a successful and fulfilling life.

210 I am deserving of all the abundance and success that I attract.

211 I am constantly setting and achieving new levels of success.

212 I am thankful for the progress I have made on my path to success.

213 I am worthy of the respect and admiration that comes with success.

214 I am proud of my own accomplishments and the accomplishments of other black men.

215 I am attracting positive and successful people into my life.

216 I am grateful for the opportunities that have allowed me to grow and succeed.

217 I am constantly moving towards the success I desire.

218 I am capable of achieving greatness and leaving a positive impact on the world.

219 I am open to new opportunities for success and growth.

220 I am grateful for the challenges that have made me stronger and wiser on my journey to success.

221 I am committed to living a life filled with success and abundance.

222 I am surrounded by people who inspire and motivate me towards success.

223 I am attracting all the resources I need to achieve my goals and succeed.

224 I am capable of overcoming any setback on my path to success.

225 I am proud of my own unique path to success and the journey that led me here.

226 I am confident in my ability to continue achieving greater success and abundance in the future.

5. 201 Powerful Positive Affirmations For Health

1 My body is strong and capable of achieving my health goals.

2 I am committed to making healthy choices every day.

3 I am worthy of prioritizing my health and well-being.

4 I choose to fuel my body with nourishing foods.

5 My body is a temple and I treat it with care and respect.

6 I am in control of my health and my life.

7 I am grateful for my body's ability to heal and regenerate.

8 I honor my body by getting enough sleep and rest.

9 I am disciplined in my exercise routine and enjoy staying active.

10 I listen to my body and give it what it needs to thrive.

11 I am grateful for the opportunity to improve my health.

12 I am worthy of feeling vibrant, energized, and healthy.

13 I love and appreciate my body for all that it does for me.

14 I trust my body's ability to heal and thrive.

15 My mind and body work together in harmony for optimal health.

16 I am resilient and capable of overcoming any health challenge.

17 I am in tune with my body's needs and respond with kindness and care.

18 My health is a top priority and I make time for self-care.

19 I am grateful for the gift of life and take care of my body accordingly.

20 I am committed to living a healthy, balanced, and fulfilling life.

21 I am capable of making positive changes to improve my health.

22 I am strong and healthy, both physically and mentally.

23 I am grateful for the abundance of nourishing food available to me.

24 I am worthy of investing time and resources into my health.

25 I honor my body by staying hydrated and nourished.

26 I am confident in my ability to make healthy choices.

27 I am deserving of a healthy and vibrant life.

28 I am worthy of feeling confident in my body and health.

29 I am grateful for my body's resilience and ability to adapt.

30 I am capable of achieving and maintaining a healthy weight.

31 I am committed to reducing stress and promoting mental well-being.

32 I am worthy of feeling comfortable in my own skin.

33 I am grateful for the positive impact exercise has on my health.

34 I am in control of my health and choose to make it a priority.

35 I am grateful for my body's ability to fight off illness and disease.

36 I am capable of creating a healthy and balanced lifestyle.

37 I am worthy of feeling strong and energized.

38 I am grateful for the resources available to me to support my health.

39 I am committed to treating my body with respect and care.

40 I am in tune with my body's signals and respond accordingly.

41 I am worthy of investing in my long-term health and well-being.

42 I am grateful for the support and encouragement of loved ones.

43 I am capable of overcoming any health obstacle that comes my way.

Positive Affirmations For Black Men

44 I am committed to maintaining healthy relationships to support my well-being.

45 I am worthy of taking time for self-care and relaxation.

46 I am grateful for the many ways my body serves me each day.

47 I am in control of my health destiny and choose to prioritize it.

48 I am capable of achieving my health goals with patience and perseverance.

49 I am worthy of feeling confident and comfortable in my body.

50 I am grateful for the many benefits of a healthy diet and lifestyle.

51 I am in control of my health destiny and choose to prioritize it.

52 I am capable of achieving my health goals with patience and perseverance.

53 I am worthy of feeling confident and comfortable in my body.

54 I am grateful for the many benefits of a healthy diet and lifestyle.

55 I am committed to prioritizing my mental and emotional well-being.

56 I am in tune with my body's signals and respond accordingly.

57 I am deserving of a long and healthy life.

58 I am capable of improving my health and wellness in meaningful ways.

59 I am grateful for my body's ability to adapt and change.

60 I am worthy of taking care of myself and my health.

61 I am committed to learning about and implementing healthy habits in my life.

62 I am confident in my ability to make positive changes to my health.

63 I am deserving of a healthy body and mind.

64 I am grateful for the opportunity to prioritize my health and well-being.

65 I am in control of my health and take responsibility for my choices.

66 I am capable of finding joy and pleasure in healthy habits.

67 I am worthy of feeling good in my own skin.

68 I am committed to creating a healthy and balanced lifestyle that works for me.

69 I am grateful for the many ways my body serves me each day.

70 I am in tune with my body's needs and respond accordingly.

71 I am deserving of a healthy and fulfilling life.

72 I am capable of overcoming any health challenge with determination and resilience.

73 I am grateful for the abundance of healthy food and resources available to me.

74 I am committed to creating a supportive environment that promotes my health.

75 I am worthy of making my health a top priority.

76 I am in control of my health and well-being, and choose to take care of myself every day.

77 I am capable of achieving my health goals with consistency and persistence.

78 I am deserving of feeling confident and empowered in my health journey.

79 I am grateful for the positive impact that exercise has on my health and well-being.

80 I am committed to taking care of myself mentally, emotionally, and physically.

81 I am in tune with my body and its signals, and honor its needs.

82 I am worthy of a happy and healthy life.

83 I am capable of making positive changes to my health that have lasting benefits.

84 I am grateful for the gift of life and the opportunity to prioritize my health.

85 I am committed to seeking out support and resources that promote my health and well-being.

86 I am in control of my health journey and trust in my ability to make positive changes.

87 I am deserving of good health and a fulfilling life.

88 I am capable of living a healthy and balanced lifestyle that brings me joy and fulfillment.

89 I am grateful for my body's ability to heal and regenerate.

90 I am committed to treating my body with respect and care, both physically and mentally.

Positive Affirmations For Black Men

91 I am in tune with my body's needs and respond with kindness and compassion.

92 I am worthy of feeling strong, energized, and healthy.

93 I am capable of finding a healthy balance that works for me and my lifestyle.

94 I am grateful for the support and encouragement of loved ones on my health journey.

95 I am committed to being patient and persistent in achieving my health goals.

96 I am in control of my health and choose to prioritize it every day.

97 I am deserving of feeling good in my own skin and I am proud of who I am.

98 I am capable of making positive choices for my health and well-being.

99 I am worthy of investing time and energy in my own health and happiness.

100 I am committed to living a long, healthy, and fulfilling life.

101 I am healthy, strong, and vibrant.

102 I feel energized and alive when I prioritize my health.

103 I am worthy of taking care of myself and feeling great.

104 I choose to honor my body and mind with healthy habits.

105 I am grateful for the ability to move my body and feel good.

106 I feel confident and empowered when I prioritize my health.

107 I am capable of achieving my health goals with consistency and commitment.

108 I feel proud of myself for prioritizing my health and well-being.

109 I am committed to living a healthy and fulfilling life.

110 I am deserving of a healthy, happy, and abundant life.

111 I feel at peace when I take care of my physical and mental health.

112 I choose to nourish my body with healthy food and movement.

113 I feel strong, capable, and resilient when I prioritize my health.

114 I am grateful for the positive impact that healthy habits have on my life.

115 I feel confident in my ability to take control of my health and well-being.

116 I am worthy of feeling good in my own skin and embracing my unique self.

117 I choose to create a healthy and balanced lifestyle that works for me.

118 I feel motivated and inspired to take care of my health every day.

119 I am capable of overcoming any health challenge with determination and resilience.

120 I feel supported and encouraged in my health journey by loved ones.

121 I am committed to creating a supportive environment that promotes my health.

122 I feel grateful for the gift of life and the opportunity to prioritize my health.

123 I am in control of my health and take responsibility for my choices.

124 I feel proud of myself for prioritizing self-care and well-being.

125 I am capable of finding joy and pleasure in healthy habits.

126 I feel deserving of a long, healthy, and fulfilling life.

127 I choose to honor my mind and body with healthy habits and self-care.

128 I feel confident in my ability to make positive changes to my health.

129 I am grateful for the abundance of healthy food and resources available to me.

130 I feel empowered to take control of my health and well-being.

131 I am committed to treating my body with respect and care, both physically and mentally.

132 I feel in tune with my body's needs and respond with kindness and compassion.

133 I am capable of creating a healthy and balanced lifestyle that brings me joy and fulfillment.

134 I feel energized and fulfilled when I prioritize my health and well-being.

135 I am deserving of a happy and healthy life.

136 I feel grateful for my body's ability to heal and regenerate.

137 I am in tune with my body's signals and respond accordingly.

138 I feel confident in my ability to find a healthy balance that works for me.

139 I am committed to seeking out support and resources that promote my health and well-being.

140 I feel worthy of feeling good in my own skin and being healthy and happy.

141 I am capable of making positive changes to my health that have lasting benefits.

142 I feel motivated to take care of my health and well-being every day.

143 I am grateful for the many benefits of a healthy diet and lifestyle.

144 I feel confident in my ability to achieve my health goals with patience and persistence.

145 I am worthy of investing time and energy in my own health and happiness.

146 I feel empowered to take control of my health and make positive changes.

147 I am committed to prioritizing my mental and emotional health as well as my physical health.

148 I feel at peace and calm when I prioritize stress-reducing habits and self-care.

149 I am capable of overcoming any obstacle that comes my way on my health journey.

150 I feel grateful for my body's ability to adapt and grow stronger with healthy habits.

151 I am worthy of feeling confident and attractive in my own body.

152 I feel inspired and motivated by my own progress and achievements.

153 I am committed to living a life filled with vitality, joy, and purpose.

154 I feel proud of myself for making positive choices that benefit my health and well-being.

155 I am deserving of a long and healthy life, filled with love and abundance.

156 I feel supported and encouraged by loved ones who want the best for my health and happiness.

157 I am capable of finding enjoyment and pleasure in healthy habits, rather than viewing them as a chore.

158 I feel confident in my ability to make positive changes to my health, no matter how small.

159 I am grateful for the many health benefits of regular exercise and movement.

160 I feel fulfilled and satisfied when I prioritize my health and well-being every day.

161 I am in control of my health, and I choose to prioritize self-care and healthy habits.

162 I feel energized and invigorated when I take care of my physical and mental health.

163 I am capable of finding balance and moderation in my lifestyle, while still prioritizing health and well-being.

164 I feel proud of myself for taking responsibility for my health and making positive choices.

165 I am worthy of feeling confident, capable, and strong in my own body.

166 I feel grateful for the gift of life, and I choose to honor it with healthy habits and self-care.

167 I am committed to seeking out resources and support that promote my health and well-being.

168 I feel motivated and inspired to take care of my health every day, no matter how small the steps may be.

169 I am deserving of a healthy, happy, and abundant life, filled with love and positivity.

170 I feel empowered to take control of my health and well-being, no matter what obstacles I may face.

171 I am capable of finding joy and pleasure in healthy habits, and creating a lifestyle that brings me happiness and fulfillment.

172 I feel confident in my ability to achieve my health goals, one step at a time.

173 I am grateful for my body's strength and resilience, and I choose to treat it with care and respect.

174 I feel at peace and calm when I prioritize healthy habits and self-care.

175 I am committed to creating a supportive environment that promotes my health and well-being.

176 I feel in tune with my body's needs, and I choose to respond with compassion and kindness.

Positive Affirmations For Black Men

177 I am capable of overcoming any health challenge with patience, persistence, and determination.

178 I feel proud of myself for making positive choices that benefit my health and happiness.

179 I am deserving of a life filled with vitality, energy, and joy.

180 I feel supported and encouraged by loved ones who want the best for my health and well-being.

181 I am committed to treating myself with kindness, love, and compassion on my health journey.

182 I feel energized and alive when I prioritize self-care and healthy habits.

183 I am worthy of feeling confident, capable, and strong in my own body and mind.

184 I feel grateful for the many benefits of a being healthy, strong, and well in the soubl body and mind.

185 I am capable of achieving my health goals with hard work and dedication.

186 I feel proud of myself for making positive changes to my health and well-being.

187 I am deserving of a life filled with happiness, joy, and good health.

188 I feel grateful for the gift of life, and I choose to honor it with healthy habits and positive actions.

189 I am committed to finding balance in my life, and prioritizing my health and well-being.

190 I feel confident in my ability to make positive changes to my lifestyle and health, no matter how small.

191 I am worthy of feeling confident, capable, and strong in my own skin.

192 I feel energized and alive when I prioritize self-care, healthy habits, and positive relationships.

193 I am committed to creating a life that brings me happiness, health, and fulfillment.

194 I feel proud of myself for taking responsibility for my health and making positive changes.

195 I am deserving of a life filled with love, positivity, and abundance.

196 I feel grateful for my body's strength and resilience, and I choose to treat it with respect and care.

197 I am capable of finding joy and pleasure in healthy habits and a healthy lifestyle.

198 I feel confident in my ability to overcome any challenge that comes my way on my health journey.

199 I am committed to finding balance and moderation in my life, while still prioritizing health and well-being.

200 I am worthy of feeling happy, fulfilled, and confident in my own skin and in my life.

201 I feel inspired and motivated by my own progress and achievements, and I am committed to continuing to improve my health and well-being.

6. 216 Powerful Positive Affirmations For Overcoming Depression

1 I am capable of overcoming my depression.

2 My mental health matters and I am taking care of it.

3 I am stronger than my depression.

4 I am worthy of love and joy.

5 I am grateful for the good things in my life.

6 I am in control of my thoughts and feelings.

7 I am taking steps to improve my mental health.

8 I am not alone in my struggles.

9 I am making progress every day.

10 I am deserving of happiness.

11 I am loved and appreciated by those around me.

12 I am creating a life that makes me happy.

13 I am learning to let go of negative thoughts.

14 I am seeking help when I need it.

15 I am stronger than my struggles.

16 I am making positive changes in my life.

17 I am capable of finding peace within myself.

18 I am practicing self-care every day.

19 I am finding joy in the small things.

20 I am learning to be kind to myself.

21 I am letting go of past traumas.

22 I am becoming a better version of myself.

23 I am taking control of my life.

24 I am finding purpose and meaning in my life.

25 I am becoming more resilient.

26 I am learning to love and accept myself.

27 I am becoming more confident in myself.

28 I am worthy of success and happiness.

29 I am letting go of things that do not serve me.

30 I am choosing to focus on the positive.

31 I am worthy of peace and contentment.

32 I am focusing on the present moment.

33 I am finding comfort in nature and the outdoors.

34 I am developing healthy coping mechanisms.

35 I am not defined by my struggles.

36 I am learning to forgive myself and others.

37 I am embracing my flaws and imperfections.

38 I am finding support in my friends and family.

39 I am learning to be patient with myself.

40 I am taking steps towards healing.

41 I am learning to be more compassionate towards myself.

42 I am capable of achieving my goals.

43 I am practicing gratitude every day.

Positive Affirmations For Black Men

44 I am taking time for myself when I need it.

45 I am focusing on my strengths.

46 I am becoming more self-aware.

47 I am learning to communicate my feelings.

48 I am seeking out positive relationships and environments.

49 I am finding peace in spirituality and faith.

50 I am letting go of the need to be perfect.

51 I am worthy of love and respect.

52 I am finding balance in my life.

53 I am embracing my creativity and passions.

54 I am capable of overcoming my obstacles.

55 I am becoming more resilient with each challenge.

56 I am finding purpose in helping others.

57 I am becoming more self-sufficient.

58 I am learning to set healthy boundaries.

59 I am finding peace in moments of stillness.

60 I am capable of creating a fulfilling life for myself.

61 I am learning to be gentle with myself.

62 I am finding strength in vulnerability.

63 I am letting go of toxic relationships and behaviors.

64 I am finding joy in the journey, not just the destination.

65 I am learning to be more present in the moment.

66 I am finding comfort in self-expression.

67 I am becoming more independent.

68 I am finding inspiration in others.

69 I am focusing on self-improvement, not comparison to others.

70 I release negative thoughts and embrace positivity and joy.

71 I choose to let go of the past and focus on the present and future.

72 I am capable of overcoming my challenges and thriving in life.

73 My mental health is a priority and I take care of myself.

74 I am deserving of love and support, and I seek it out when needed.

75 I am a strong and resilient person, and I am proud of who I am.

76 I am grateful for the small blessings in my life and find joy in them.

77 I allow myself to feel and express my emotions in a healthy way.

78 I am learning and growing every day, and I am proud of my progress.

79 I am surrounded by positivity, love, and support.

80 I am capable of achieving my goals and dreams.

81 I am valuable and appreciated by those around me.

82 I choose to focus on the good in my life and let go of negativity.

83 I am not alone in my struggles and I seek out support when needed.

84 I am capable of overcoming my fears and living my best life.

85 I am grateful for my life and the people in it.

86 I am proud of who I am and what I have accomplished.

87 I am worthy of love, happiness, and success.

88 I am in control of my thoughts and emotions, and I choose positivity.

89 I am grateful for each day and the opportunities it brings.

90 I am surrounded by positive energy and love.

91 I am capable of creating the life I want to live.

92 I am confident in my abilities and talents.

93 I embrace my imperfections and see them as strengths.

94 I am grateful for the support and encouragement of those around me.

95 I am capable of achieving my goals and overcoming obstacles.

96 I am strong and resilient, and I can handle any challenges that come my way.

97 I am grateful for the progress I have made in my life and mental health.

Positive Affirmations For Black Men

98 I am proud of myself for taking steps towards healing and recovery.

99 I am surrounded by people who uplift and support me.

100 I have the courage and strength to face my challenges.

101 I am worthy of love and respect, and I give it to myself first.

102 I am grateful for the lessons I have learned in my journey.

103 I am capable of forgiving myself and others.

104 I am resilient and can bounce back from any setbacks.

105 I am worthy of peace, joy, and fulfillment.

106 I choose to let go of negativity and focus on positivity.

107 I am grateful for the progress I have made in my mental health journey.

108 I am capable of creating a life full of happiness and purpose.

109 I am capable of overcoming my fears and doubts.

110 I am surrounded by people who believe in me and my potential.

111 I am deserving of kindness, respect, and compassion.

112 I am capable of achieving anything I set my mind to.

113 I am proud of the progress I have made in my healing journey.

114 I am grateful for the support and encouragement of my loved ones.

115 I am worthy of a life full of love, joy, and abundance.

116 I am strong and resilient, and I can handle anything life throws my way.

117 I am worthy of love and happiness.

118 I am strong and capable of overcoming any challenge.

119 I am not defined by my past or my struggles.

120 I choose to focus on the positive things in my life.

121 I deserve to feel good about myself and my life.

122 I am allowed to ask for help when I need it.

123 I am in control of my thoughts and emotions.

124 I am capable of healing and growing.

125 I am surrounded by people who love and support me.

126 I am a work in progress, and that's okay.

127 I trust myself to make the right decisions for my life.

128 I am worthy of respect and kindness from myself and others.

129 I am open to new opportunities for growth and healing.

130 I choose to let go of negative thoughts and emotions.

131 I am allowed to make mistakes and learn from them.

132 I am strong enough to face my challenges and overcome them.

133 I am worthy of happiness and peace of mind.

134 I am a valuable member of my community and have something to offer.

135 I am kind and compassionate towards myself and others.

136 I am deserving of success and fulfillment.

137 I am in charge of my own happiness and well-being.

138 I am worthy of love and respect from others.

139 I am deserving of forgiveness and second chances.

140 I am grateful for the people in my life who support and encourage me.

141 I am allowed to set boundaries to protect my mental health.

142 I am worthy of taking care of myself and my needs.

143 I am capable of finding joy and pleasure in life.

144 I am in control of my own destiny and future.

145 I am allowed to prioritize my mental health and well-being.

146 I am worthy of the effort it takes to heal and grow.

147 I am grateful for the experiences that have shaped me into who I am today.

148 I am capable of bouncing back from setbacks and challenges.

149 I am surrounded by beauty and positivity in the world around me.

150 I am deserving of rest and self-care.

151 I am capable of making positive changes in my life.

Positive Affirmations For Black Men

152 I am allowed to feel my emotions and express them in healthy ways.

153 I am worthy of respect and recognition for my accomplishments.

154 I am grateful for the support and encouragement of others.

155 I am strong enough to handle whatever comes my way.

156 I am deserving of peace and happiness in my life.

157 I am capable of overcoming my fears and anxieties.

158 I am in control of my own happiness and fulfillment.

159 I am allowed to take time for myself and my own needs.

160 I am worthy of love and affection from myself and others.

161 I am capable of learning and growing from my mistakes.

162 I am surrounded by abundance and positivity in my life.

163 I am grateful for the progress I have made in my healing journey.

164 I am allowed to feel hopeful and optimistic about the future.

165 I am worthy of love and support from others.

166 I am capable of achieving a life of happiness and fulfillment.

167 I am in control of my own thoughts and emotions.

168 I am allowed to seek help and support from others when I need it.

169 I am worthy of feeling good about myself and my accomplishments.

170 I am deserving of happiness and peace.

171 I am worthy of love and support.

172 I am strong and resilient.

173 I am capable of overcoming any obstacle.

174 I am healing and growing every day.

175 I choose to focus on positive thoughts and feelings.

176 I have the power to change my mindset.

177 I am letting go of negativity and embracing positivity.

178 I am living in the present moment and finding joy in small things.

179 I am accepting myself and my emotions.

180 I am proud of my progress and growth.

181 I am surrounded by people who care about me and support me.

182 I am learning to love myself unconditionally.

183 I am grateful for my life and the opportunities it offers.

184 I am letting go of shame and guilt.

185 I am embracing self-care and self-compassion.

186 I am creating a life filled with joy and purpose.

187 I am a valuable and important member of my community.

188 I am not alone in my struggles and challenges.

189 I am building a strong foundation for my mental health and wellbeing.

190 I am open to seeking help and support when I need it.

191 I am finding hope and inspiration in the world around me.

192 I am cultivating healthy and supportive relationships.

193 I am taking care of my physical health to support my mental health.

194 I am committed to my journey of healing and growth.

195 I am learning to communicate my needs and feelings effectively.

196 I am letting go of perfectionism and embracing imperfection.

197 I am finding peace and comfort in nature.

198 I am forgiving myself and others for past mistakes and hurts.

199 I am creating a life that aligns with my values and passions.

200 I am proud of myself for seeking help and support.

201 I am learning to set healthy boundaries for myself.

202 I am taking ownership of my mental health and wellbeing.

203 I am resilient and able to bounce back from challenges.

204 I am learning to cope with stress in healthy ways.

205 I am grateful for the people and things that bring me joy and happiness.

Positive Affirmations For Black Men

206 I am not defined by my mental health challenges.

207 I am worthy of love and respect, regardless of my struggles.

208 I am building a life filled with balance and harmony.

209 I am making progress, even if it feels slow at times.

210 I am embracing vulnerability and authenticity.

211 I am learning to be gentle and kind to myself.

212 I am worthy of rest and relaxation.

213 I am finding beauty and meaning in my experiences.

214 I am learning to let go of negative self-talk and embrace positive affirmations.

215 I am capable of achieving inner peace and happiness.

216 I am deserving of a life filled with joy, purpose, and fulfillment.

7. 448 Powerful Positive Affirmations For Self-Esteem

1 My life is full of love.

2 I am confident in my ability to navigate difficult situations with grace and resilience.

3 I embrace my unique individuality.

4 I have a lot to offer the world, and I am excited to share my gifts with others.

5 I have come this far, and I can keep going.

6 Others accept and love me for who I am.

7 I send love to my fears and doubts.

8 I believe in my own ability to create positive change in the world.

9 I am proud of my own creativity and imagination.

10 I have a positive and healing effect on others.

11 I believe in my own potential for greatness.

12 I am confident in my ability to learn and grow from my mistakes.

13 All of my decisions are inspired from inner wisdom and compassion.

14 I am proud of who I am and what I have accomplished.

Positive Affirmations For Black Men

15 I am who I need to be.

16 I am worthy of success and happiness.

17 I am authentic, true, and expressive.

18 I let my love for myself increase each day.

19 I am deserving of love.

20 I will stand my ground and defend myself.

21 I am whole.

22 I am proud of the person I am becoming.

23 I am blessed.

24 I am capable of reaching my goals.

25 I trust myself to make the right decisions for my life.

26 I carry strength and resilience with me.

27 I am capable of achieving anything I set my mind to.

28 I am valued.

29 I am a radiant and joyous person.

30 I am confident in my individuality.

31 I choose to see the good in myself and in others.

32 My confidence is soaring

33 I choose to see challenges as opportunities for growth and development.

34 Every part of my body radiates beauty.

35 My unique qualities make me special and valuable.

36 I am a unique and valuable individual with much to offer the world.

37 I am a healer, of my own life and of others.

38 I am blanketed in the Universes' loving energy.

39 I am proud of the positive impact I have on the world around me.

40 I let go of those who do not have my best interests at heart.

41 I am a juggernaut, unstoppable in the pursuit of my goals.

42 I overcome challenges with grace and ease.

43 I have always and will continue to always try my best; I honor this.

44 I am exuberant and filled with love for who I am.

45 I am proud of my integrity and honesty.

46 I am a titan of industry, making waves and shaping the world.

47 I am a jackhammer, breaking down any obstacle in my way.

48 I am proud of who I am and the person I am becoming.

49 I have a lot to offer the world.

50 My unique talents and abilities are worthy of recognition and praise.

51 My individuality is important.

52 I am worthy of respect and admiration from others.

53 The love within me flows through me in every situation.

54 Loving myself comes easily and naturally.

55 I have a caring heart.

56 I am not defined by my mistakes or failures.

57 I am worthy of being seen and heard.

58 I am deserving of love, care, and affection.

59 I am proud of myself.

60 I am confident in my ability to communicate effectively and assertively.

61 I am capable of achieving great things, and I will not let doubt hold me back.

62 I am confident in my ability to express myself honestly and openly.

63 I am a leader and a role model for others to look up to.

64 Everything I need is within me.

65 I am surrounded by love and positivity, and I attract the people and opportunities that align with my values.

66 I trust my instincts and follow my heart.

Positive Affirmations For Black Men

67 I am confident in my ability to slay any challenge.

68 I have achieved great things.

69 I am worthy of all the good things life has to offer.

70 I radiate confidence.

71 I am a role model for others, and I lead by example with my positive attitude and actions.

72 I am a wizard of words, with the power to inspire and uplift.

73 I am not defined by my past mistakes or failures.

74 I have a warm and caring heart.

75 I am worthy of receiving love and affection from others.

76 I am comfortable in my own skin and embrace my unique qualities.

77 I am proud of the person I am and the journey that has led me here.

78 I love the woman/man that I am.

79 I have the power to create a life that brings me joy.

80 I deserve good things.

81 I am confident in my ability to make a positive impact in the world.

82 I am a genius, capable of incredible feats.

83 I love the person I am becoming.

84 I am the architect of my own success story.

85 I am worthy of success and recognition for my hard work.

86 I have everything I need.

87 I am deserving of happiness and fulfillment, and I will not settle for anything less.

88 I am capable of overcoming any obstacle or challenge, and I have a resilient spirit.

89 I am confident in my abilities and trust myself to make the right decisions.

90 I am capable of loving fully and completely.

91 I am worthy of love.

92 I am confident and self-assured, and I am not afraid to take risks or try new things.

93 I choose to nourish my health.

94 I am capable of expressing my emotions in healthy and constructive ways.

95 I am a shining star, destined for greatness.

96 I believe in my own unique strengths and qualities.

97 I radiate love.

98 I trust in my ability to survive and thrive through any obstacle.

99 I celebrate my many successes.

100 I am powerful and in control of my own destiny.

101 I choose to focus on my strengths and build upon them.

102 I am deserving of rest and relaxation, and I prioritize my mental and physical health.

103 I am a work of art.

104 I will care for myself as much as I care for others.

105 I am a conductor, orchestrating my life with precision.

106 I am proud of my own unique perspective on the world.

107 I am confident in my ability to learn and grow.

108 I am comfortable in my own skin and confident in my own abilities.

109 I believe in my own capacity for growth and self-improvement.

110 I am a knight, protecting and serving those in need.

111 I am a good person who deserves good things in life.

112 I deserve to be happy and fulfilled.

113 I am deserving of success and abundance in all areas of my life.

114 I deflect negativity.

115 I am a work in progress, and I am proud of the person I am becoming.

Positive Affirmations For Black Men

116 I am capable of building and maintaining positive and healthy relationships.

117 I am capable of finding joy and beauty in the world around me.

118 I am committed to taking care of myself both physically and mentally.

119 My struggles are just opportunities to learn.

120 I am proud of my unique perspectives and ideas.

121 I am grateful for all of the blessings in my life.

122 I can achieve anything I set my mind to.

123 I am constantly pushing myself to new heights and achieving my goals.

124 I am worthy of happiness and joy in my life.

125 I trust my own intuition and inner wisdom.

126 My inner beauty shines brightly.

127 I walk this world with grace.

128 I deserve happiness.

129 I am confident and assured in all that I do.

130 I am a wise owl with the knowledge to navigate any obstacle.

131 I am a superhero, with the power to save the day.

132 I am not defined by my past mistakes or failures, and I have the power to create a better future for myself.

133 I am constantly growing and improving.

134 I am open to receive love.

135 I will focus on the bright side.

136 I am a positive influence on those around me, and I uplift and inspire others.

137 I am worthy of positive and fulfilling relationships.

138 I am confident in my abilities and talents, and I am not afraid to show them off.

139 I choose to stop apologizing for being me.

140 Today, I choose myself.

141 I am worthy of all the good things that come into my life.

142 I am deserving of respect and recognition for my personal boundaries and limits.

143 I am deserving of respect and recognition for my accomplishments.

144 I have a loving relationship with my body.

145 I believe in my own strength and resilience.

146 I am a boss, making moves and taking charge of my life.

147 I am deserving of forgiveness and compassion for myself and others.

148 I am confident in my abilities and skills.

149 I am a strong and capable person who can handle anything that comes my way.

150 I have so much to celebrate in life.

151 I trust my intuition.

152 I am pure beauty.

153 I am always learning and growing.

154 I am a diamond-in-the-rough, all I need is some polishing.

155 I trust in my own instincts and abilities to make good decisions.

156 I am constantly growing and improving as a person.

157 I am grounded, peaceful, and centered.

158 I honor and respect my limitations.

159 Compassion is infinite and fully surrounds me and my life.

160 Negativity has no place in my life.

161 I choose to see the good in myself and others, and approach life with a positive outlook.

162 I choose to focus on the good in myself and others, and let go of negativity.

163 I am a top-notch performer, excelling in everything I do.

164 Abundance and love flow from me.

165 I love the body I was born with.

Positive Affirmations For Black Men

166 I am a powerful force of positivity in the world.

167 I am worthy of love and respect, and I will not settle for less.

168 My life is full of happiness and love.

169 I am a champion with the strength to win any battle.

170 I believe in my own power to make a positive impact in the world.

171 I choose to believe in myself and my abilities, and know that I can accomplish anything I set my mind to.

172 I have a lot to offer the world, and I embrace my potential.

173 I am deserving of all the blessings that come into my life.

174 I am always learning and growing, and I embrace new experiences and challenges.

175 I let go of my past and live in the present.

176 I have the ability to overcome any challenge life gives me.

177 I believe in my own potential to achieve my dreams and goals.

178 I practice self-compassion when I do not succeed.

179 Today I start loving myself more.

180 I am a trendsetter, blazing a path for others to follow.

181 I am worthy of love, peace, and joy.

182 I am an adventurer with a thirst for life.

183 I am strong and resilient.

184 I am blessed with many talents and abilities that make me unique and special.

185 I am proud of my unique talents and abilities, and I share them with the world.

186 I am cocooned in the loving energy of the Universe.

187 I am deserving of respect and and deep admiration from friends family and society.

188 My life is filled with love and joy.

189 My life is founded on respect for myself and others.

190 I attract positive and loving people into my life.

191 I have the power to create the life I want.

192 I am not the sum of my mistakes.

193 I am the healer of my own life.

194 I stand my ground and protect myself with compassionate assertiveness.

195 I am capable of achieving my goals and dreams.

196 Success is defined by my willingness to keep going.

197 I am proud of the person I am today and the person I am becoming.

198 I am a wizard, creating magic in every aspect of my life.

199 Love rises from my heart in the face of difficulty.

200 I am capable of overcoming any challenge that comes my way.

201 I allow myself to feel deeply.

202 I believe in the person I dream of becoming.

203 I embrace my flaws, knowing no one is perfect.

204 I am capable of achieving any goal that I set my mind to.

205 I am open-minded and accepting of different perspectives and ideas.

206 I am deserving of success, and I will not let setbacks or failures discourage me.

207 The only approval I need is my own.

208 I am deserving of success and happiness in all areas of my life.

209 I am not my negative thoughts or emotions.

210 I believe in my own worth and value as a person.

211 I honor and respect my limitations and thank myself for the capabilities I do have.

212 I attract love and light.

213 I reward myself for my hard work and dedication.

214 I feel profound empathy and love for others and their own unique paths.

215 My body is a beautiful expression of my individuality.

Positive Affirmations For Black Men

216 I am worthy of love and affection from myself and others.

217 I am a superhero with the ability to conquer anything.

218 Life is filled with joy and abundance.

219 I love my body and all it does for me.

220 I am in control of my happiness.

221 I am worthy of infinite and unending compassion.

222 I am proud of my resilience and ability to bounce back from setbacks.

223 I am resilient and capable of bouncing back from setbacks.

224 I am centered, peaceful, and grounded.

225 I am proud of my heritage and the contributions of my community to society.

226 I am a motivator, inspiring greatness in others.

227 I am always learning and expanding my knowledge and skills.

228 I am capable of standing up for myself and advocating for my own needs.

229 I feel beautiful, I am beautiful.

230 I release any need for suffering.

231 I am confident in my ability to make positive changes in my life.

232 I am an important and valuable contributor to society, and I am proud of my contributions.

233 I did not get up today to "just" be average. I will excel.

234 I will be assertive when I need to be.

235 I am confident in my ability to handle challenges and obstacles.

236 I am powerful, confident, and capable of reaching all my dreams.

237 I am not defined by the expectations of others, and I trust my own judgment.

238 I can say no when something does not serve me.

239 I am capable of creating my own destiny.

240 I am blessed with many wonderful qualities and characteristics.

241 I do not let my fears hold me back.

242 Love flows from within me.

243 I deserve love, compassion, and empathy.

244 I am confident in who I am and what I bring to the table.

245 I am deserving of love and respect.

246 I am worthy of success and prosperity.

247 I am resilient and able to bounce back from any challenge or setback.

248 I am whole alone.

249 I am committed to my personal growth and development.

250 I am a miracle worker, creating magic wherever I go.

251 I am powerful and confident.

252 I am grateful for all that I have and all that I am.

253 I am deserving of love, support, and care from the important people in my life.

254 I am deserving of respect and admiration for all that I am.

255 I am proud of my heritage and culture.

256 I am strong, resilient, and determined.

257 I am comfortable setting boundaries and saying no when necessary.

258 I am becoming more prosperous every day.

259 I treat my body with love and care.

260 I am deserving of positive relationships that uplift and support me.

261 I let go of that which no longer serves me.

262 I am capable and confident in my abilities.

263 I am a bulldozer, clearing the path for my success.

264 I am a social butterfly, connecting with others and building relationships.

265 I love my own company.

266 I am deserving of peace and harmony in my life.

267 I am valuable and contribute positively to the world around me.

Positive Affirmations For Black Men

268 I am at peace with all that has happened in my life.

269 I am capable of creating the life I desire, and I take action towards my goals every day.

270 I can choose self-love whenever I desire.

271 I am a titan of technology, advancing the world with my innovations.

272 I am a trailblazer, paving the way for others to follow.

273 I am comfortable in my own skin and embrace my uniqueness.

274 I am balanced.

275 I am worthy of acceptance and love for who I am.

276 I embrace my strengths and weaknesses, and use them to my advantage.

277 I am kind to myself.

278 I am capable of achieving success and happiness in all areas of my life.

279 I choose to focus on my strengths and talents.

280 I am capable of creating a life that brings me joy and fulfillment.

281 I am a guru, with the knowledge and wisdom to create a fulfilling life.

282 I am worthy of forgiveness and second chances.

283 I am grateful for all that I have in my life.

284 Happiness flows freely from me.

285 I am not my mistakes or my flaws.

286 Life gives me opportunities for success and achievement in the ways I desire.

287 I have so much to love about myself.

288 I am worthy of love and respect.

289 I am loved.

290 I am confident in my ability to set and achieve my goals.

291 I love and accept all of me.

292 I am a beautiful person.

293 I respect myself.

Daberechi N

294 I am proud of my accomplishments and achievements.

295 My decisions are based on inner wisdom.

296 I am love incarnated.

297 My life is a reflection of the love inside me.

298 I trust in my own self-worth and value as a person.

299 I trust myself to make the right decisions.

300 I am confident in my ability to communicate my thoughts and ideas effectively.

301 I love the person that I am.

302 I am a unique and valuable individual, and I celebrate my differences.

303 I am the king of my own destiny.

304 Self-love comes to me with ease.

305 I make time to care for myself.

306 I trust that I can handle whatever comes my way.

307 I have the strength to rise in the face of adversity.

308 My life is filled with joy and abundance.

309 I am capable of making the changes necessary to live my best life.

310 My capacity for love is infinite.

311 I am a wise owl, with the insight to navigate any challenge.

312 I have all I need to live a happy life.

313 I am proud of who I am and all that I have accomplished.

314 I trust in my own strength and resilience to overcome challenges.

315 The more I practice loving myself, the more lovable I become.

316 I am a good listener and communicator, and I cultivate healthy and fulfilling relationships.

317 I am capable of making positive changes in my life and the lives of those around me.

318 I radiate confidence and self-assurance in all that I do.

Positive Affirmations For Black Men

319 I am a rockstar in my own right.

320 The universe supports me, always.

321 Today, I choose me.

322 I am comfortable in my own skin, and I love and accept myself for who I am.

323 I have faith in my abilities.

324 I am comfortable expressing my thoughts and emotions.

325 I am worthy of infinite compassion.

326 I am worthy of being treated with kindness and compassion.

327 I am worthy of respect and admiration, and I carry myself with confidence and dignity.

328 Love brings me youthfulness, energy, and rejuvenates me.

329 I am deserving of kindness and compassion from myself and others.

330 I choose to let go of negative self-talk and embrace positivity.

331 I accept compliments easily.

332 I am enough just the way I am, and I don't need to prove myself to anyone.

333 I love every part of what makes me who I am.

334 feel pride in myself.

335 I am a smooth operator, handling any situation with ease.

336 I am confident in my ability to adapt to new situations and environments.

337 I am unstoppable in the pursuit of my dreams.

338 I have infinite capacity for love and affection.

339 I am in control of my own actions.

340 I am a visionary, with the ability to see beyond what is possible.

341 I will not take criticism personally.

342 I am capable of showing up authentically and genuinely in all of my relationships.

343 Loving myself means I am able to love others more.

344 I have a strong sense of purpose and meaning in my life, and I am motivated to achieve my goals.

345 My inner world creates my outer world.

346 I am capable of creating a life filled with joy and abundance.

347 I am a shining example of excellence and greatness.

348 I am always growing and improving, and I am proud of the progress I have made.

349 I am committed to living a life that aligns with my values and beliefs.

350 I am worthy of admiration and respect from myself and others.

351 I prioritize myself and my needs.

352 I overflow with creativity and good ideas.

353 I am increasing my prosperity every day.

354 I am proud of my unique talents and gifts.

355 My body is my best friend.

356 I have the power to change my world.

357 I love and treasure my body.

358 I am deserving of the good things that come my way in life.

359 I deserve love.

360 Happiness flows from me.

361 My life is full of endless opportunities for success and happiness.

362 I am proud of my accomplishments, no matter how big or small, and I celebrate my progress.

363 I am capable of achieving my wildest dreams and desires.

364 My life is a place of balance and harmony.

365 I am a valuable member of my community, and I make a positive impact in the world.

366 I deserve the good that happens to me.

367 I let go of negative self talk.

Positive Affirmations For Black Men

368 My life is a celebration of my accomplishments.

369 I choose to view my life positively.

370 I am a warrior, standing strong in the face of adversity.

371 I choose to embrace my strengths and work on my weaknesses.

372 I am proud of my cultural heritage and identity.

373 I am empowered to create change in my life.

374 I forgive myself and learn from my mistakes.

375 I am a champion of change, creating a better world.

376 I am proud of the person I am today, and I am excited to see the person I will become in the future.

377 I am grateful for all that I have.

378 I am a master of my craft, honing my skills with precision.

379 I am constantly striving to be the best version of myself.

380 I have a positive attitude and a can-do spirit, and I approach every challenge with confidence.

381 I do not judge myself or others.

382 I do not need anyone to feel worthy.

383 I am a sage, with the wisdom to navigate any situation.

384 I believe in myself.

385 I am a jack of all trades, capable of mastering anything I put my mind to.

386 I am a rockstar, living life to the fullest and embracing adventure.

387 I am willing to keep going, when things get tough, to achieve the success I deserve

388 I am loved and appreciated for who I am, not just what I do.

389 I respect my own boundaries.

390 I trust my own judgement and decision-making skills.

391 I release the need to judge myself negatively.

392 I am loved beyond comprehension.

393 I am a star athlete, dominating the game with my skills.

394 I believe in my own potential and ability to succeed.

395 I am proud of my own individuality and sense of self.

396 I am the master of my own happiness.

397 I appreciate the people in my life who support and uplift me, and I am grateful for their presence.

398 I am a beacon of light in the darkness.

399 I am capable of overcoming any fear or self-doubt that may arise.

400 I am in control of my thoughts and emotions, and I choose to focus on the positive.

401 I am growing each and every day.

402 My mind is filled with loving thoughts.

403 I am surrounded by positive and supportive people who believe in me.

404 I am successful.

405 I choose to focus on my strengths and accomplishments.

406 I am love.

407 Love flows freely from inside of me.

408 I trust my intuition and make choices that align with my values and goals.

409 I am worthy of kindness, compassion, and understanding.

410 My self-worth is not determined by external factors.

411 I am a lionheart, with the courage to take on anything.

412 I follow my own expectations, not the expectations of others.

413 I let love in.

414 I am enough.

415 I am confident in my abilities and talents.

416 I am not defined by my mistakes, and I have the power to choose a new direction for my life.

417 I have worth and inner beauty.

Positive Affirmations For Black Men

418 I am deserving of respect and admiration.

419 My body is beautiful and expresses my spirit.

420 I am a master of my domain, in control of my life and destiny.

421 I am deserving of happiness and fulfillment in all areas of my life.

422 I am exactly who I need to be in this moment.

423 I am confident in my ability to overcome challenges and obstacles.

424 I am a magician, turning dreams into reality.

425 I am confident and strong.

426 I am deserving of love, success, and happiness, and I will not settle for anything less.

427 I am deserving of love and respect from myself and others.

428 I honor my own life path.

429 I am a beacon of hope, inspiring those around me.

430 I am grateful for everything I have and everything I am.

431 I am a lion, fierce and fearless.

432 I am more than my body.

433 I deserve success and happiness.

434 I have always and will always try my best.

435 I am constantly learning and growing as a person.

436 I am deserving of respect and recognition for my hard work and accomplishments.

437 I control my fears, they do not control me.

438 I am beautiful, inside and out.

439 I am a king among men, deserving of respect and admiration.

440 I am confident in my decisions and choices.

441 My every step is one of courage.

442 I trust in my ability to make it through difficult times.

443 I trust in my own intuition and inner guidance.

444 I trust in my own ability to persevere and overcome adversity.

445 I am a valuable asset to my community.

446 I am proud of my achievements and accomplishments.

447 I accept myself unconditionally.

448 I am confident in my ability to handle difficult situations.

8. 201 Powerful Positive Affirmations For Anxiety

1 I am capable of managing my anxiety and finding peace within myself.

2 I am deserving of a life free from anxiety and filled with positivity and joy.

3 I feel empowered to take control of my thoughts and emotions.

4 I am worthy of feeling calm, relaxed, and centered.

5 I choose to focus on the present moment and let go of worries about the future.

6 I feel strong and capable when I face my fears and overcome them.

7 I am committed to seeking support and help when I need it, and that is a sign of strength.

8 I am capable of learning and implementing healthy coping mechanisms to manage my anxiety.

9 I am deserving of a peaceful mind and a calm spirit.

10 I feel grateful for the moments of peace and clarity I experience, and I strive to create more of them.

11 I am worthy of feeling confident and in control of my own emotions and thoughts.

12 I am committed to seeking out positive experiences and focusing on the good in my life.

13 I feel empowered to face my anxiety head-on and work towards a healthier and more fulfilling life.

14 I am capable of finding peace and happiness, even in the midst of anxiety and stress.

15 I am deserving of a life that is filled with love, positivity, and hope.

16 I choose to let go of negative self-talk and focus on positive affirmations and thoughts.

17 I feel confident in my ability to manage my anxiety and take care of myself.

18 I am committed to finding healthy outlets for my stress and anxiety, such as exercise or mindfulness practices.

19 I am worthy of feeling calm, centered, and at peace with myself and the world around me.

20 I feel grateful for the love and support of my friends and family, and I am empowered to seek their help when I need it.

21 I am capable of finding joy and happiness in my life, even when anxiety threatens to take it away.

22 I am deserving of a life that is free from anxiety and filled with positive experiences.

23 I feel strong and capable when I overcome my fears and take control of my anxiety.

24 I am committed to practicing self-care and nurturing my own well-being, both physically and mentally.

25 I am worthy of feeling loved, valued, and appreciated, even in the midst of anxiety and stress.

26 I feel empowered to make positive changes in my life and overcome the obstacles that stand in my way.

27 I am capable of finding peace and tranquility in my life, even in the midst of chaos and turmoil.

28 I am deserving of a life that is filled with purpose, meaning, and joy.

29 I feel confident in my ability to manage my anxiety and maintain a healthy mindset.

Positive Affirmations For Black Men

30 I am committed to finding healthy ways to manage my stress and anxiety, such as therapy or meditation.

31 I am worthy of feeling calm, centered, and balanced in my own life and relationships.

32 I feel grateful for the love and support of my community, and I am empowered to seek out that support when I need it.

33 I am capable of finding happiness and fulfillment in my life, even when anxiety threatens to take it away.

34 I am deserving of a life that is free from anxiety and filled with positive opportunities.

35 I feel strong and capable when I overcome my fears and take action towards a better life.

36 I am committed to taking care of myself and nurturing my own well-being, both physically and mentally.

37 I am worthy of feeling confident, successful, and fulfilled in my life and my relationships.

38 I feel empowered to make positive changes in my life and break free from the cycle of anxiety and stress.

39 I am capable of finding inner strength and resilience in the face of anxiety and fear.

40 I am deserving of a life that is filled with happiness, success, and fulfillment.

41 I am committed to practicing self-love and compassion in order to overcome my anxiety.

42 I am worthy of feeling peaceful, calm, and centered in my life and relationships.

43 I feel empowered to take action towards a healthier and more positive future.

44 I am capable of finding hope and positivity even in the darkest of times.

45 I am deserving of a life that is filled with love, laughter, and joy.

46 I feel strong and capable when I take control of my thoughts and emotions.

47 I am committed to seeking out positive experiences and opportunities for growth and self-improvement.

48 I am worthy of feeling confident, successful, and fulfilled in my personal and professional life.

49 I feel grateful for the supportive and caring people in my life who help me manage my anxiety.

50 I am capable of finding peace and tranquility in the midst of chaos and uncertainty.

51 I am deserving of a life that is free from anxiety and filled with positive relationships and experiences.

52 I feel confident in my ability to manage my anxiety and maintain a healthy and balanced life.

53 I am committed to finding healthy outlets for my stress and anxiety, such as exercise or creative expression.

54 I feel empowered to seek help and support when I need it, and to ask for what I need in order to manage my anxiety.

55 I am capable of finding happiness and fulfillment in my life, even when anxiety threatens to hold me back.

56 I am deserving of a life that is filled with purpose, meaning, and positivity.

57 I am committed to taking care of my physical and mental health in order to overcome my anxiety.

58 I am worthy of feeling confident, successful, and fulfilled in all areas of my life.

59 I feel grateful for the moments of peace and clarity that I experience, and I strive to create more of them.

60 I am capable of finding inner peace and calm, even in the midst of anxiety and stress.

61 I am deserving of a life that is free from anxiety and filled with positive energy and experiences.

62 I feel confident in my ability to manage my anxiety and take control of my thoughts and emotions.

63 I am committed to seeking out healthy and positive relationships in my life, and to letting go of toxic or negative influences.

64 I am worthy of feeling loved, valued, and appreciated by those around me.

Positive Affirmations For Black Men

65 I feel empowered to face my anxiety head-on and take action towards a healthier and happier life.

66 I am deserving of a life that is filled with positivity, hope, and love.

67 I feel strong and capable when I practice self-care and prioritize my own well-being.

68 I am committed to finding healthy ways to manage my anxiety, such as therapy or meditation.

69 I am worthy of feeling calm, centered, and in control of my own thoughts and emotions.

70 I feel confident in my ability to face my fears and move beyond them.

71 I am in control of my thoughts and emotions.

72 My mind is calm and at peace.

73 I release all worries and fears, and welcome calmness and positivity.

74 I choose to focus on the present moment and find joy in it.

75 I am capable of handling any situation that comes my way.

76 I trust in my inner strength and resilience.

77 I choose to let go of negative thoughts and replace them with positive ones.

78 I am surrounded by love and support from family and friends.

79 I am grateful for all the positive things in my life.

80 I am worthy of love and respect, and I treat myself with kindness.

81 I am worthy of happiness and success, and I embrace all opportunities that come my way.

82 I am stronger than my anxiety, and I refuse to let it control me.

83 I am at peace with myself and the world around me.

84 I trust in my ability to overcome any challenges and obstacles.

85 I am confident in myself and my abilities.

86 I trust in the process of life, and know that everything will work out for my highest good.

Daberechi N

87 I am filled with positive energy and joy.

88 I choose to focus on the good in every situation.

89 I am surrounded by positivity and abundance.

90 I am in tune with my body and my emotions.

91 I am free from anxiety and worry.

92 I am confident and at ease in social situations.

93 I am worthy of love and acceptance, and I love and accept myself.

94 I am grateful for the opportunities and experiences in my life.

95 I am in control of my breathing and use it to calm myself.

96 I am surrounded by people who love and support me.

97 I trust in my intuition and make decisions with confidence.

98 I choose to live in the present moment and enjoy it fully.

99 I am free from fear and worry, and embrace life with open arms.

100 I am worthy of success and abundance, and I embrace it fully.

101 I choose to see the good in every situation and find joy in it.

102 I am confident in my abilities and trust in my instincts.

103 I am capable of achieving my goals and dreams.

104 I am surrounded by positive energy and joy.

105 I am worthy of love and respect, and I treat myself with kindness and compassion.

106 I am surrounded by people who uplift and support me.

107 I am grateful for all the blessings in my life.

108 I am capable of managing my thoughts and emotions.

109 I am at ease and comfortable in any situation.

110 I am worthy of happiness and success, and I attract it into my life.

111 I am strong and resilient, and can overcome any obstacle.

112 I choose to let go of negative thoughts and emotions, and welcome positivity.

Positive Affirmations For Black Men

113 I am in control of my thoughts and choose to focus on the good in life.

114 I am confident and comfortable in my own skin.

115 I am surrounded by love and positive energy.

116 I trust in the journey of life, and embrace it fully.

117 I am capable of achieving anything I set my mind to.

118 I am surrounded by people who inspire and motivate me.

119 I am in control of my life and my destiny.

120 I am free from anxiety and worry, and embrace life with open arms.

121 I trust that I have the strength to overcome my anxiety.

122 I am capable of finding peace and calm in any situation.

123 I choose to release all anxiety and embrace a sense of calm.

124 My mind is clear and free from anxiety.

125 I have the power to control my thoughts and emotions.

126 I am worthy of living a life free from anxiety.

127 I trust in my ability to overcome my fears and anxieties.

128 I choose to focus on the present moment, and let go of worries about the future.

129 I release all anxiety from my mind and body, and welcome in peace and tranquility.

130 I am surrounded by positive energy and thoughts, which help to alleviate my anxiety.

131 I trust that I can manage any anxiety that comes my way.

132 I am in control of my thoughts and emotions, and I choose to let go of any anxious feelings.

133 I am surrounded by love and support, which helps me to overcome my anxiety.

134 My mind is calm and at ease, and I am able to approach every situation with confidence.

135 I am strong, and I have the ability to conquer my fears and anxieties.

136 I trust in the universe to guide me towards a life free from anxiety.

137 I am capable of finding joy and happiness, even in the midst of anxiety.

138 I choose to embrace a positive mindset and release all anxiety from my thoughts.

139 I am worthy of feeling calm and at ease in every aspect of my life.

140 My mind is a peaceful oasis, free from anxiety and worry.

141 I am surrounded by positive energy and thoughts that help me to overcome anxiety.

142 I trust that I can manage my anxiety and overcome any obstacles that come my way.

143 I am strong and capable of managing any anxious thoughts or feelings.

144 I choose to focus on the present moment, and let go of worries about the past.

145 I release all anxiety and embrace a sense of calm and peace.

146 I trust in my ability to navigate through anxious situations with grace and ease.

147 I am surrounded by a network of supportive people who help me to overcome my anxiety.

148 My mind is at ease and I am able to approach every situation with a clear head.

149 I choose to let go of anxious thoughts and embrace a positive, optimistic mindset.

150 I am worthy of feeling calm, confident, and in control in every aspect of my life.

151 I trust in my ability to manage my anxiety, and approach every situation with confidence.

152 I am capable of finding peace and calm in even the most stressful situations.

153 I am surrounded by positivity and love, which helps to alleviate my anxiety.

154 I choose to focus on my strengths and release all anxiety from my thoughts.

Positive Affirmations For Black Men

155 I trust in my ability to overcome my fears and anxieties, and to live a life of joy and abundance.

156 I am in control of my thoughts and emotions, and I choose to let go of anxious feelings.

157 I am worthy of feeling calm and at ease in every situation, no matter how challenging.

158 My mind is clear, and I am able to approach every situation with clarity and focus.

159 I choose to embrace a positive mindset, and let go of anxious thoughts and feelings.

160 I am surrounded by a supportive network of people who help me to overcome my anxiety.

161 I trust that I am capable of managing my anxiety and living a life free from fear.

162 I am strong and resilient, and I can overcome any obstacle that comes my way.

163 I am capable of handling any challenges that come my way.

164 I trust in my ability to overcome anxiety and live a fulfilling life.

165 I choose to focus on positive thoughts and let go of negative ones.

166 I am grateful for the good things in my life and choose to focus on them.

167 I am worthy of love and acceptance, including self-love and self-acceptance.

168 I trust in my inner strength and resilience to overcome anxiety.

169 I am patient and kind with myself as I work through my anxiety.

170 I am strong and capable of overcoming any anxiety or fear.

171 I am not alone in my struggles and there are people who care about me and want to support me.

172 I choose to believe in my own power to overcome anxiety and live a fulfilling life.

173 I am learning to take things one step at a time and not let anxiety overwhelm me.

174 I am capable of achieving my goals and dreams, even if anxiety tries to hold me back.

175 I am open to new experiences and opportunities, even if they make me feel anxious at first.

176 I am stronger than any anxiety I may feel and I will not let it control my life.

177 I have the power to change my thoughts and transform my anxious feelings into positive ones.

178 I am kind to myself and give myself permission to rest and recharge when needed.

179 I am proud of myself for the progress I have made in overcoming anxiety.

180 I am committed to my own well-being and will take steps to prioritize self-care and stress management.

181 I choose to live a life of peace, happiness, and freedom from anxiety.

182 I am calm, cool, and collected, even in the face of anxiety.

183 I am in control of my thoughts and emotions, and anxiety has no power over me.

184 Anxiety may knock at my door, but I won't let it in.

185 I am more powerful than my anxiety, and I can overcome it.

186 I am stronger than my anxiety, and I will rise above it.

187 I choose to focus on the positive, and anxiety fades away.

188 My mind is a calm oasis, and anxiety cannot disturb it.

189 I am a warrior, and anxiety is my defeated foe.

190 Anxiety is no match for my determination and resilience.

191 I release my anxiety and embrace peace and serenity.

192 I breathe in calmness and exhale anxiety.

193 I am at peace with myself and my surroundings, and anxiety has no place here.

194 I am relaxed, confident, and free from anxiety.

195 I choose to live in the present moment, and anxiety cannot follow me there.

Positive Affirmations For Black Men

196 I am in charge of my mind, and I choose to think positively.

197 I am centered, balanced, and free from anxiety's grip.

198 I am full of joy and optimism, and anxiety cannot steal it from me.

199 I am in control of my breath, and anxiety cannot control me.

200 I am grateful for each day, and anxiety cannot ruin my appreciation for life.

201 I am cool, calm, and collected, and anxiety has no place in my life.

9. 206 Powerful Positive Affirmations For Relationships

1 I am worthy of love and respect in all of my relationships.

2 I deserve to be with someone who accepts me for who I am.

3 I am attracting loving and supportive relationships into my life.

4 My relationship is getting stronger every day.

5 I am grateful for the love and support that I receive from my partner.

6 I am a good listener and communicator in my relationship.

7 I trust my partner and feel secure in our relationship.

8 I am able to express my needs and feelings in a healthy way.

9 My partner and I are growing and evolving together.

10 I am committed to making my relationship work.

11 I choose to focus on the positive aspects of my relationship.

12 I am able to forgive and move on from past mistakes in my relationship.

13 I bring happiness and joy to my partner's life.

14 My partner and I have a deep emotional connection.

15 I am attracting a partner who shares my values and goals.

16 I am patient and understanding in my relationship.

Positive Affirmations For Black Men

17 I am able to handle conflicts in a calm and respectful manner.

18 I am attracting a partner who is kind and compassionate.

19 My relationship is based on mutual love, trust, and respect.

20 I am able to balance my personal and relationship needs.

21 I am constantly learning and growing in my relationship.

22 I am open to receiving love and affection from my partner.

23 My relationship is filled with passion and intimacy.

24 I am committed to being loyal and faithful to my partner.

25 I am worthy of a happy and fulfilling relationship.

26 I am attracting a partner who makes me feel appreciated and valued.

27 My relationship is a source of support and encouragement for me.

28 I am able to let go of any past relationship baggage and move forward.

29 I am able to maintain healthy boundaries in my relationship.

30 I am able to express my love and affection for my partner.

31 I am able to communicate my needs and desires in a clear and confident manner.

32 My partner and I are building a strong foundation for our future together.

33 I am able to see my partner's perspective and work towards a mutual understanding.

34 I am able to compromise when necessary in my relationship.

35 My relationship is filled with laughter and joy.

36 I am worthy of a loving and committed partner.

37 I am able to trust and be vulnerable with my partner.

38 My relationship is built on a strong emotional connection.

39 I am able to provide emotional support and encouragement to my partner.

40 I am able to let go of any negative relationship patterns and embrace healthy ones.

41 I am able to create a safe and nurturing environment for my partner.

42 My partner and I are able to work through any challenges that arise in our relationship.

43 I am able to show my partner love and appreciation every day.

44 My relationship is a source of happiness and fulfillment in my life.

45 I am able to communicate my love and affection for my partner in a variety of ways.

46 My partner and I are able to grow and learn together.

47 I am able to support my partner's goals and dreams.

48 I am able to show empathy and understanding towards my partner.

49 My relationship is filled with trust, honesty, and transparency.

50 I am attracting a partner who is loyal, supportive, and caring.

51 My relationship is a source of strength and stability for me.

52 I am able to let go of any insecurities or fears that may harm my relationship.

53 I am worthy of love and respect in my relationships.

54 I am open to healthy and supportive relationships.

55 My relationships are built on trust, honesty, and communication.

56 I am able to give and receive love in a healthy way.

57 I attract positive and loving people into my life.

58 My relationships are fulfilling and satisfying.

59 I am committed to growth and improvement in my relationships.

60 I am patient and understanding with my partner.

61 I am able to forgive and let go of past hurts in my relationships.

62 I am grateful for the love and support I receive from my partner.

63 I prioritize quality time with my partner to strengthen our connection.

64 I am able to express my needs and desires in my relationships.

65 I am confident in my ability to maintain healthy and positive relationships.

66 My partner and I support each other's goals and dreams.

67 I am able to create a strong and lasting bond with my partner.

Positive Affirmations For Black Men

68 I am deserving of a loving and respectful partner.

69 I choose to focus on the positive aspects of my relationships.

70 My relationships are a source of joy and fulfillment in my life.

71 I am willing to work through challenges and conflicts in my relationships.

72 I am able to maintain a healthy balance between my individuality and my relationship.

73 I am capable of building a deep emotional connection with my partner.

74 My partner and I communicate openly and honestly with each other.

75 I am committed to creating a loving and harmonious home life with my partner.

76 I am able to provide emotional support and care to my partner.

77 I am grateful for the positive impact my partner has on my life.

78 I am deserving of a partner who values and respects me.

79 I am able to maintain a sense of independence and autonomy within my relationship.

80 My partner and I share common values and beliefs.

81 I choose to see the best in my partner and appreciate their positive qualities.

82 I am capable of having a fulfilling and happy romantic relationship.

83 I am able to maintain a sense of fun and playfulness in my relationship.

84 I am committed to creating a strong and lasting partnership with my significant other.

85 I am able to communicate my love and affection to my partner.

86 I am able to trust and rely on my partner in a healthy way.

87 I am deserving of a loving and supportive partner who encourages my growth and development.

88 I am able to create a strong and positive family dynamic with my partner.

89 I am able to work through any issues or challenges that arise in my relationships.

90 I am capable of having a deep and meaningful connection with my partner.

91 I am able to express my feelings and emotions in a healthy way to my partner.

92 My relationship is a safe and supportive space for me to be myself.

93 I am able to provide emotional and physical intimacy to my partner.

94 I am committed to building a healthy and happy relationship with my partner.

95 My partner and I are able to grow and evolve together.

96 I am willing to put in the time and effort necessary to maintain a healthy relationship.

97 I am able to have open and honest communication with my partner.

98 I am deserving of a relationship that is built on mutual love and respect.

99 My partner and I are able to build a life of happiness and fulfillment together.

100 I am able to support and encourage my partner's personal and professional growth.

101 I am deserving of a loving and supportive relationship.

102 I am worthy of a partner who respects and cherishes me.

103 I am capable of building a strong and healthy relationship.

104 I am willing to put in the effort to make my relationship thrive.

105 I am open to giving and receiving love in my relationship.

106 I feel a deep connection with my partner.

107 I trust my partner to always have my best interests at heart.

108 I feel safe and secure in my relationship.

109 I am grateful for the love and companionship of my partner.

110 I am committed to working through challenges in my relationship.

111 I am capable of communicating my needs and feelings effectively in my relationship.

112 I am willing to compromise and find solutions that work for both me and my partner.

113 I feel understood and appreciated by my partner.

114 I am willing to forgive and let go of past mistakes in my relationship.

Positive Affirmations For Black Men

115 I am able to express my love and affection for my partner freely and openly.

116 I feel empowered and supported by my partner.

117 I am able to balance my individual needs with the needs of my relationship.

118 I am committed to building a long-lasting and fulfilling relationship.

119 I am open to learning and growing with my partner.

120 I feel a deep sense of belonging and connection in my relationship.

121 I am able to express my emotions and vulnerability with my partner.

122 I am able to fully trust and rely on my partner.

123 I feel valued and appreciated by my partner.

124 I am able to show my partner love and appreciation in meaningful ways.

125 I am willing to put in the time and effort to maintain a healthy and loving relationship.

126 I am able to express my opinions and ideas freely in my relationship.

127 I am able to maintain a healthy balance of independence and togetherness in my relationship.

128 I feel a deep sense of love and gratitude for my partner.

129 I am willing to work through conflicts and disagreements in a respectful and constructive manner.

130 I am able to prioritize and make time for my relationship.

131 I am able to show my partner love and affection in a way that resonates with them.

132 I am able to create a strong emotional connection with my partner.

133 I am willing to support and encourage my partner in their goals and dreams.

134 I am able to balance intimacy and emotional connection in my relationship.

135 I am able to communicate and navigate boundaries effectively in my relationship.

136 I feel supported and uplifted by my partner.

137 I am willing to take responsibility for my actions and mistakes in my relationship.

138 I am able to create and maintain a sense of fun and playfulness in my relationship.

139 I am able to prioritize my partner's needs and feelings in my relationship.

140 I am able to create a sense of stability and security in my relationship.

141 I feel a deep sense of respect and admiration for my partner.

142 I am able to show my partner empathy and understanding.

143 I am able to communicate my appreciation for my partner in a way that resonates with them.

144 I am able to make compromises that benefit both me and my partner.

145 I feel a deep sense of intimacy and connection in my relationship.

146 I am able to be vulnerable and open with my partner.

147 I am deserving of love and respect in my relationships.

148 I choose to attract positive and uplifting people into my life.

149 I am capable of being vulnerable with my partner and expressing my emotions.

150 My relationship is a safe space where I can be myself and grow.

151 I am grateful for the love and support of my partner.

152 My partner and I communicate effectively and openly.

153 My relationship is based on mutual respect and understanding.

154 I am committed to making my relationship a priority.

155 I choose to approach conflicts in my relationship with compassion and understanding.

156 I trust in the strength of my relationship to overcome any obstacles.

157 My partner and I share a deep and meaningful connection.

158 I am a loving and attentive partner.

159 I am confident in my ability to maintain a healthy and fulfilling relationship.

160 I am deserving of love, and I choose to accept it fully.

161 My relationship is a source of joy and fulfillment in my life.

Positive Affirmations For Black Men

162 I am capable of creating a strong and healthy partnership.

163 My partner and I support each other's growth and development.

164 I am open to receiving love in all forms.

165 I trust in the longevity and stability of my relationship.

166 I am deserving of a loving and fulfilling partnership, and I choose to manifest it in my life.

167 My partner and I share a deep and unbreakable bond.

168 I am open to giving and receiving love in equal measure.

169 My relationship is based on honesty and trust.

170 I am grateful for the positive impact that my partner has on my life.

171 My relationship is a reflection of the love and care that I put into it.

172 I am committed to creating a stable and secure relationship.

173 My partner and I create a balance of independence and togetherness.

174 I choose to surround myself with supportive and loving relationships.

175 I am worthy of love and affection in my relationship.

176 My partner and I share a deep emotional connection that strengthens over time.

177 I am confident in my ability to communicate my needs and boundaries in my relationship.

178 My relationship is a source of positivity and happiness in my life.

179 I choose to create a relationship that is full of trust and respect.

180 I am capable of creating a loving and nurturing home environment.

181 I am deserving of a partnership that supports my goals and aspirations.

182 My relationship is built on a foundation of mutual love and admiration.

183 I am grateful for the positive impact that my partner has on my mental and emotional well-being.

184 My relationship brings out the best in me, and I bring out the best in my partner.

185 I trust in the health and longevity of my relationship.

Daberechi N

186 I am capable of navigating any challenges that arise in my relationship with grace and understanding.

187 My partner and I communicate in a way that fosters intimacy and closeness.

188 I am deserving of a relationship that is full of joy and fulfillment.

189 I choose to create a relationship that is grounded in respect, trust, and compassion.

190 My relationship is a place where I can let my guard down and be my authentic self.

191 I am capable of nurturing and growing my relationship over time.

192 I am grateful for the love and support that my partner provides to me.

193 My relationship is a constant source of happiness and positivity in my life.

194 I trust in the natural ebb and flow of my relationship.

195 I choose to create a relationship that is full of mutual support and encouragement.

196 I am worthy of a loving and fulfilling relationship.

197 I attract positive and healthy relationships into my life.

198 My relationships are built on a foundation of trust and respect.

199 I communicate my needs and desires clearly and respectfully in my relationships.

200 I am grateful for the love and support I receive from my partner and loved ones.

201 I am committed to continuously learning and growing within my relationships.

202 I am deserving of a partner who supports and uplifts me.

203 I release any negative beliefs or patterns that may hinder my relationships.

204 I approach my relationships with an open heart and mind.

205 I radiate positive energy and attract positive relationships into my life.

206 I am deserving of a relationship that brings me joy, peace, and happiness.

10. 245 Powerful Positive Affirmations For Confidence

1 I am confident in my ability to create wealth and abundance.

2 I am worthy of success and abundance.

3 I am deserving of wealth and prosperity.

4 I have the power to create the financial life I desire.

5 I trust in my ability to attract wealth and success.

6 I am confident in my knowledge and skills to create wealth.

7 I am a magnet for wealth and abundance.

8 I am grateful for the abundance in my life.

9 I am open to receiving wealth and prosperity.

10 I am confident in my ability to manage my finances.

11 I am worthy of financial security and stability.

12 I trust in my ability to make smart financial decisions.

13 I am deserving of financial freedom and independence.

14 I am grateful for the opportunities that bring me wealth and abundance.

15 I am confident in my ability to grow my wealth and investments.

16 I am worthy of the financial rewards of my hard work and dedication.

17 I trust in my ability to build and grow my wealth.

18 I am deserving of a life of financial comfort and security.

19 I am open to receiving new opportunities for wealth and abundance.

20 I am grateful for the financial abundance in my life.

21 I am confident in my ability to make wise financial decisions.

22 I am worthy of financial abundance and prosperity.

23 I trust in my ability to manage my wealth with wisdom and clarity.

24 I am deserving of the best life that wealth can offer.

25 I am open to new ideas and opportunities for wealth and success.

26 I am grateful for the financial abundance that comes my way.

27 I am confident in my ability to create and grow my wealth.

28 I am worthy of the rewards of my hard work and dedication.

29 I trust in my ability to make sound financial decisions.

30 I am deserving of a life of financial abundance and prosperity.

31 I am open to receiving the blessings of wealth and success.

32 I am confident in my ability to manage and grow my finances.

33 I am worthy of a life of financial security and freedom.

34 I trust in my ability to attract and create wealth and abundance.

35 I am deserving of the financial rewards that come with my success.

36 I am open to new opportunities for wealth and prosperity.

37 I am grateful for the wealth and abundance in my life.

38 I am confident in my ability to create a life of financial abundance.

39 I am worthy of a life of luxury and financial freedom.

40 I trust in my ability to manage and grow my wealth with ease.

41 I am deserving of a life of financial comfort and stability.

42 I am open to receiving the rewards of wealth and success.

43 I am grateful for the financial abundance that flows to me.

Positive Affirmations For Black Men

44 I am confident in my ability to create and grow my wealth with joy.

45 I am worthy of a life of financial independence and freedom.

46 I trust in my ability to attract the wealth and success I desire.

47 I am deserving of a life of abundance and prosperity.

48 I am open to the unlimited possibilities of wealth and success.

49 I am grateful for the financial abundance that enriches my life.

50 I am confident in my ability to make the most of my financial opportunities.

51 I am worthy of the rewards that come with my financial success.

52 I trust in my ability to make smart and profitable investments.

53 I am deserving of a life of wealth and financial stability.

54 I attract wealth and abundance effortlessly.

55 My financial goals are achievable, and I am taking the necessary steps to reach them.

56 Wealth and prosperity flow into my life naturally.

57 I am worthy of financial success and abundance.

58 My financial success inspires others around me.

59 I am confident in my ability to manage my finances wisely.

60 I am financially independent and secure.

61 I am open to receiving all the wealth and abundance the universe has to offer.

62 I am creating a life of financial freedom for myself and my loved ones.

63 I am smart and capable of making sound financial decisions.

64 I am deserving of all the good things that come my way.

65 I trust the universe to guide me towards financial success.

66 I am attracting opportunities for wealth and abundance into my life.

67 I am committed to growing my wealth and achieving financial freedom.

68 I have the courage to take risks that lead to financial rewards.

69 I am capable of achieving any financial goal I set for myself.

70 I am grateful for the financial abundance in my life, both big and small.

71 I am confident in my ability to create a successful financial future.

72 I am in control of my finances and making smart financial decisions.

73 I am surrounded by positive energy that supports my financial success.

74 My mindset is focused on financial abundance and success.

75 I am confident in my ability to earn, save, and invest wisely.

76 I am attracting financial opportunities that align with my values and goals.

77 I am worthy of experiencing financial abundance and success.

78 I have the skills and knowledge necessary to build and grow my wealth.

79 I am creating a life of financial abundance and freedom for myself and my family.

80 My financial success is a reflection of my hard work and dedication.

81 I am capable of overcoming any financial challenge that comes my way.

82 I trust myself to make wise financial decisions that lead to success.

83 I am focused on achieving my financial goals with confidence and ease.

84 I am a magnet for wealth and prosperity.

85 I am worthy of receiving unlimited financial abundance in my life.

86 I am confident in my ability to create and maintain a successful financial future.

87 I am open to learning and growing my financial knowledge and skills.

88 I am grateful for the financial opportunities that come my way.

89 My financial success inspires and uplifts others around me.

90 I am capable of creating a life of financial abundance and joy.

91 I trust the universe to guide me towards financial freedom and success.

92 I am surrounded by positive influences that support my financial growth and success.

93 I am confident in my ability to create multiple streams of income.

94 I am grateful for all the financial blessings in my life.

Positive Affirmations For Black Men

95 I am creating a legacy of financial abundance and success for future generations.

96 I trust myself to make wise investment decisions that lead to financial growth.

97 I am worthy of experiencing unlimited financial prosperity in my life.

98 I am surrounded by opportunities for financial growth and success.

99 My financial goals are achievable, and I am taking daily action towards them.

100 I am grateful for my financial abundance and excited for what the future holds.

101 I am creating a life of financial freedom that allows me to pursue my passions.

102 I am confident in my ability to achieve any financial goal I set for myself.

103 I radiate confidence and positive energy.

104 I am bold, fearless, and unstoppable.

105 I trust my abilities to achieve anything I desire.

106 I am confident in my unique strengths and talents.

107 I love and accept myself fully, just as I am.

108 I am the master of my thoughts and emotions.

109 I believe in myself and my potential to create greatness.

110 I am a confident and charismatic communicator.

111 I am capable of handling any challenge that comes my way.

112 I am open to new opportunities and experiences.

113 I am confident in my ability to learn and grow.

114 I am worthy of love, respect, and admiration.

115 I radiate success and positivity in everything I do.

116 I have the power to create the life I want.

117 I am confident in my ability to make sound decisions.

118 I am surrounded by positive and supportive people.

119 I am grateful for all my talents and blessings.

120 I am worthy of achieving my dreams and goals.

121 I am a confident and capable leader.

122 I trust myself to handle any situation with grace and ease.

123 I am worthy of receiving all the good that life has to offer.

124 I am confident in my ability to overcome any obstacle.

125 I am a magnet for success and positive opportunities.

126 I am grateful for all the abundance and wealth in my life.

127 I am confident in my ability to inspire and uplift others.

128 I radiate confidence, strength, and resilience.

129 I am worthy of living a life filled with joy and happiness.

130 I am confident in my ability to take risks and try new things.

131 I am capable of achieving all my goals and dreams.

132 I am worthy of living a life of purpose and fulfillment.

133 I trust my intuition and inner wisdom.

134 I am confident in my ability to create a life of abundance and prosperity.

135 I am worthy of all the success and happiness in the world.

136 I radiate confidence and positive vibes wherever I go.

137 I am confident in my ability to handle any challenge with ease and grace.

138 I trust myself to make wise and empowering decisions.

139 I am surrounded by abundance, prosperity, and wealth.

140 I am confident in my ability to create a life I love.

141 I am worthy of achieving all my financial goals and dreams.

142 I am a confident and successful entrepreneur.

143 I am grateful for all the abundance and prosperity in my life.

144 I am confident in my ability to attract wealth and abundance.

145 I trust my abilities to make my dreams a reality.

146 I am confident in my ability to achieve financial freedom.

Positive Affirmations For Black Men

147 I am worthy of creating a life of wealth and prosperity.

148 I radiate confidence, strength, and power in everything I do.

149 I am confident in my ability to build wealth and prosperity for myself and others.

150 I am worthy of living a life of financial abundance and security.

151 I trust my intuition and inner guidance to make smart financial decisions.

152 I am confident in my ability to create a life of financial freedom and independence.

153 I am surrounded by positive and successful people who support my goals and dreams.

154 I am grateful for all the opportunities and blessings in my life.

155 I am capable of achieving great things and nothing can stop me.

156 I radiate confidence and positivity in everything that I do.

157 I am proud of my accomplishments and eager to take on new challenges.

158 I am confident in my ability to handle any situation that comes my way.

159 My confidence grows stronger every day.

160 I believe in myself and my ability to make my dreams a reality.

161 I trust my instincts and make decisions with confidence and clarity.

162 I exude confidence and attract success in all areas of my life.

163 I am confident in my ability to overcome any obstacle and emerge victorious.

164 My confidence empowers me to take risks and seize new opportunities.

165 I trust in my abilities and embrace challenges as opportunities for growth.

166 I am confident in my worth and know that I deserve the best that life has to offer.

167 I am fearless in the pursuit of my goals and dreams.

168 My confidence is contagious and inspires those around me.

169 I am confident in my skills and abilities to achieve my goals.

170 I have unwavering faith in my ability to create the life I desire.

171 I am confident in my ability to learn and grow from every experience.

172 My confidence allows me to take bold and decisive action towards my goals.

173 I believe in my ability to create the life I desire and deserve.

174 I am filled with boundless confidence and determination.

175 I embrace my unique talents and use them to achieve success.

176 I am confident in my ability to overcome any challenge that comes my way.

177 My confidence allows me to create abundance and success in all areas of my life.

178 I am confident in my ability to handle any situation with grace and ease.

179 I believe in my potential to achieve greatness and leave a positive impact on the world.

180 My confidence is a powerful force that propels me towards success.

181 I trust in myself and my ability to make sound decisions for my life.

182 I am confident in my ability to attract and create the life that I desire.

183 I radiate confidence and attract positive and supportive people into my life.

184 I am confident in my unique strengths and talents and use them to achieve my goals.

185 I trust in the journey of my life and have unwavering faith in my ability to succeed.

186 I am confident in my ability to handle any challenge that comes my way with ease and grace.

187 I believe in my potential to achieve success beyond my wildest dreams.

188 My confidence is an unstoppable force that leads me towards my goals.

189 I am worthy of success, abundance, and happiness.

190 I trust in my ability to create a life of my dreams and am confident in my ability to make it happen.

191 I am filled with unbreakable confidence that allows me to tackle any challenge with ease.

192 I am worthy of love, respect, and admiration, and have the confidence to receive it.

Positive Affirmations For Black Men

193 My confidence is unwavering and empowers me to achieve great things.

194 I am confident in my ability to create a life of joy, prosperity, and abundance.

195 I have the power to create a life that is fulfilling, abundant, and full of joy.

196 I trust in my ability to manifest my deepest desires and create the life I want to live.

197 I am confident in my ability to take bold and inspired action towards my goals.

198 Confidence comes naturally to me.

199 I trust my abilities and know that I can handle any challenge.

200 I believe in myself and my vision.

201 Every day, I am becoming more confident.

202 I am grateful for all the experiences that have helped me grow in confidence.

203 I am worthy of success and happiness.

204 I am confident in my own skin and embrace my uniqueness.

205 I am proud of my accomplishments and continue to achieve more.

206 I am strong, capable, and confident.

207 I am confident in my decisions and trust my intuition.

208 I am comfortable speaking my mind and expressing myself.

209 I am confident in my abilities and trust myself to succeed.

210 I am confident in my skills and knowledge, and always eager to learn more.

211 I am in control of my thoughts and emotions, and choose to focus on positivity and confidence.

212 I am becoming more confident with each passing day.

213 I am confident in my ability to adapt to any situation.

214 I am confident in my intelligence and problem-solving skills.

215 I am confident in my ability to connect with others and build positive relationships.

216 I am confident in my ability to create the life I want to live.

217 I am confident in my value and worth.

218 I am confident in my ability to set and achieve my goals.

219 I am confident in my creativity and ability to think outside the box.

220 I am confident in my ability to handle rejection and turn it into motivation.

221 I am confident in my ability to persevere and overcome obstacles.

222 I am confident in my ability to learn from my mistakes and grow.

223 I am confident in my ability to lead and inspire others.

224 I am confident in my ability to make a positive impact on the world.

225 I am confident in my ability to find opportunities and create success.

226 I am confident in my ability to adapt and thrive in any situation.

227 I am confident in my ability to embrace change and make it work for me.

228 I am confident in my ability to overcome fear and take risks.

229 I am confident in my ability to handle criticism and use it constructively.

230 I am confident in my ability to communicate effectively and assertively.

231 I am confident in my ability to listen actively and show empathy.

232 I am confident in my ability to forgive and let go of negativity.

233 I am confident in my ability to be honest and authentic.

234 I am confident in my ability to maintain healthy boundaries and prioritize my well-being.

235 I am confident in my ability to stay motivated and persevere through challenges.

236 I am confident in my ability to find joy and positivity in every situation.

237 I am confident in my ability to make the right choices for myself.

238 I am confident in my ability to trust and rely on myself.

239 I am confident in my ability to be kind to myself and practice self-compassion.

240 I am confident in my ability to handle conflict in a positive and productive way.

Positive Affirmations For Black Men

241 I am confident in my ability to take action and make progress towards my goals.

242 I am confident in my ability to be successful and achieve my dreams.

243 I am confident in my ability to make a difference in the world.

244 I am confident in my ability to live a fulfilling and joyful life.

245 I am confident in my ability to find solutions and think creatively.

11. 215 Powerful Positive Affirmations For Love

1 I am worthy of love and affection.

2 I am deserving of a healthy and loving relationship.

3 I radiate love and attract it effortlessly.

4 I am a magnet for positive and fulfilling relationships.

5 Love comes to me easily and effortlessly.

6 I am attracting the perfect partner into my life.

7 I am surrounded by love and support.

8 I open myself to give and receive love fully and fearlessly.

9 I am a great catch, and someone amazing is looking for me.

10 I am confident in my ability to give and receive love.

11 I am lovable and loving.

12 I am attracting my soulmate, and I trust the universe's timing.

13 I am worthy of a partner who values and cherishes me.

14 I am capable of creating a healthy and loving relationship.

15 I am ready and open to love and be loved.

16 I am deserving of a partner who accepts and supports me unconditionally.

Positive Affirmations For Black Men

17 Love flows to me naturally and easily.

18 I am attracting the love that I desire and deserve.

19 I am open and receptive to new and exciting experiences.

20 I am attracting a partner who makes me feel valued and appreciated.

21 I am worthy of love and respect from my partner.

22 I am capable of giving and receiving love in healthy ways.

23 I am surrounded by love, peace, and happiness.

24 I am confident in my ability to create a strong and fulfilling relationship.

25 I trust my intuition to guide me to the right partner.

26 I am capable of resolving conflicts in a healthy and loving way.

27 I am deserving of a partner who shares similar values and interests.

28 I am open to the possibility of falling deeply in love.

29 I am worthy of a partner who sees and appreciates my unique qualities.

30 I am capable of building a strong and healthy relationship with my partner.

31 I am attracting the partner who is best suited for me.

32 I am ready and willing to commit to a loving and fulfilling relationship.

33 I am attracting love and positivity into my life.

34 I am worthy of being loved unconditionally.

35 I am capable of creating a loving and nurturing environment in my relationships.

36 I am a great partner, and my qualities attract the perfect match.

37 I am deserving of love and happiness in all areas of my life.

38 I trust that the universe is working in my favor to bring me the perfect partner.

39 I am worthy of being loved for who I am.

40 I am attracting a partner who supports and encourages my dreams and goals.

41 I am confident in my ability to be vulnerable in my relationships.

42 I am open to the beauty and magic of love.

43 I am attracting a partner who is emotionally available and committed to our relationship.

44 I am worthy of being treated with kindness and respect in my relationships.

45 I am capable of creating a strong foundation for my relationships.

46 I am open and receptive to the love that is already present in my life.

47 I am capable of giving and receiving love unconditionally.

48 I am deserving of a partner who values my time and energy.

49 I am confident in my ability to create a healthy and fulfilling relationship.

50 I am open and receptive to the love that surrounds me.

51 I am attracting a partner who shares my passions and interests.

52 I am worthy of love that is patient, kind, and understanding.

53 I am worthy of love and I attract it effortlessly.

54 I open my heart to receive love and all the joy it brings.

55 My love is valuable and appreciated.

56 I am proud of the love I give and receive.

57 I attract healthy and fulfilling relationships.

58 I am deserving of the deepest love, and I accept it into my life.

59 I am open to love and ready for a healthy relationship.

60 I trust my heart to lead me to the right person.

61 I have a generous and loving spirit that is attractive to others.

62 Love flows to me and through me easily and effortlessly.

63 I am constantly growing and evolving in my capacity to love.

64 I am deserving of love and respect, and I attract partners who give me both.

65 I am confident in myself and in my ability to attract and maintain healthy relationships.

66 I am grateful for the love that I have in my life, and I nurture it daily.

67 I choose to be vulnerable and open to love, even when it's scary.

68 I radiate love and it comes back to me tenfold.

Positive Affirmations For Black Men

69 I am capable of giving and receiving love in all its forms.

70 I embrace the journey of love and all the lessons it teaches me.

71 I am open to all the wonderful possibilities that love brings into my life.

72 Love is abundant, and I am worthy of all its blessings.

73 I am comfortable expressing my love for others, and I do so freely.

74 I attract love by being authentic and true to myself.

75 I choose to focus on the positive aspects of love and let go of any fears or doubts.

76 I am worthy of being loved exactly as I am, flaws and all.

77 I am grateful for the love that I have experienced in the past and look forward to even more in the future.

78 I am constantly learning and growing in my ability to give and receive love.

79 I attract healthy and loving partners who are right for me.

80 I am patient and trust that the right person will come into my life at the right time.

81 Love is a beautiful adventure, and I am excited to experience it fully.

82 I am filled with love, and that love spills over into all areas of my life.

83 I am surrounded by love, and I attract even more of it each day.

84 I am comfortable with intimacy and am capable of forming deep connections with others.

85 I choose to let go of any past hurt or pain, and open myself up to new love and new possibilities.

86 Love is my natural state, and I feel it deeply within my heart.

87 I am confident in my ability to show love to others in ways that are meaningful and appreciated.

88 I am deserving of a loving and healthy relationship, and I am open to receiving it.

89 I am grateful for the love and support of family and friends, and cherish those connections.

90 I choose to believe in the power of love to transform my life and the lives of others.

91 I am proud of the love I give and receive, and celebrate it every day.

92 Love is my birthright, and I claim it fully and joyfully.

93 I am confident in my ability to overcome any challenges that arise in my relationships.

94 I am worthy of being cherished and adored by a loving partner.

95 Love is a beautiful and necessary part of my life, and I welcome it with open arms.

96 I trust my instincts and my heart to guide me towards love and happiness.

97 I am deserving of love and respect.

98 Love flows effortlessly into my life.

99 I am open and receptive to love.

100 My heart is overflowing with love and positivity.

101 My relationships are always filled with love and support.

102 I attract loving, kind, and compassionate people into my life.

103 Love is abundant and always available to me.

104 I am a magnet for love and positive energy.

105 I am worthy of the love and happiness I desire.

106 I am surrounded by loving and supportive friends and family.

107 Love is a beautiful and transformative force in my life.

108 I am capable of giving and receiving love in equal measure.

109 My heart is open and ready to receive the love that is meant for me.

110 I choose to see love in every situation and in every person I meet.

111 I am filled with love and radiate positivity to those around me.

112 Love is the foundation of all my relationships.

113 I attract love and happiness by being my authentic self.

114 My love is a gift that I give freely to those around me.

Positive Affirmations For Black Men

115 I am grateful for the love and support I receive from my loved ones.

116 Love is the most powerful force in the universe, and it is within me.

117 I am lovable and deserving of love.

118 I radiate love and attract it easily.

119 Love comes naturally to me, and I am open to receiving it.

120 I am worthy of a healthy and fulfilling relationship.

121 My heart is open and ready to give and receive love.

122 I choose to see the good in people and let love in.

123 I am grateful for the love in my life and excited for more to come.

124 Love brings me joy and happiness.

125 I am loved for who I am, flaws and all.

126 My love is powerful and makes a positive impact on the world.

127 Love flows to me in abundance, and I share it generously.

128 My heart is full of love and light.

129 I attract loving and respectful people into my life.

130 Love fills me up and makes me feel alive.

131 I am worthy of being cherished and adored.

132 Love is a beautiful adventure, and I am excited to explore it.

133 I trust in the power of love to heal and transform.

134 I am a magnet for healthy, fulfilling relationships.

135 Love connects me to others and to my higher self.

136 I am deserving of unconditional love and acceptance.

137 I am surrounded by love and positivity, and it lifts me up.

138 Love makes everything better and more meaningful.

139 I am open to giving and receiving love in all forms.

140 I am whole and complete, and love is an added bonus to my life.

141 I am grateful for the love that surrounds me and fills my heart.

142 Love is my superpower, and I use it to create a better world.

143 I am blessed with love from family, friends, and partners.

144 I give and receive love freely and without fear.

145 Love is the foundation of all that is good in my life.

146 I embrace love and let it guide my actions and decisions.

147 I am worthy of a deep and meaningful love.

148 My heart is open and ready to receive the love I deserve.

149 Love makes me feel alive and empowered.

150 I attract love effortlessly and with ease.

151 Love is a gift that I cherish and appreciate every day.

152 I am grateful for the love that has come into my life and for what is yet to come.

153 I am a loving and caring person, and that energy attracts more love to me.

154 I am surrounded by people who love and support me unconditionally.

155 Love is a never-ending source of inspiration and motivation for me.

156 I am worthy of all the love that the universe has to offer.

157 Love gives me the courage to be my authentic self and follow my passions.

158 My heart is overflowing with love, and it touches everyone I meet.

159 I am grateful for the lessons that love has taught me and for the growth it has brought me.

160 Love is the energy that fuels my dreams and aspirations.

161 I am a magnet for love, joy, and abundance.

162 My heart is open, and I am ready to give and receive love.

163 Love is a beautiful journey that I am excited to take.

164 I am deserving of the highest form of love, and I am willing to wait for it.

165 I am surrounded by love, and it helps me to overcome challenges.

166 Love is the greatest force in the universe, and it is always available to me.

Positive Affirmations For Black Men

167 I am grateful for the love that surrounds me and fills my life with joy and happiness.

168 I am worthy of love and affection just the way I am.

169 I am surrounded by love and support from my family and friends.

170 Love flows easily to me and through me.

171 I am a magnet for love and I attract loving people and situations.

172 I am open to receiving love and I accept it with gratitude.

173 Love is my natural state and it feels great.

174 I am filled with love and it radiates from me.

175 Love empowers me and gives me the courage to face any challenge.

176 I am loved and cherished by those around me.

177 I am surrounded by loving and caring people who lift me up.

178 Love comes to me effortlessly and abundantly.

179 I am worthy of unconditional love and support.

180 I am open to love and I trust the journey of love.

181 I am deserving of true and genuine love.

182 I am grateful for the love in my life and I cherish it deeply.

183 My heart is full of love and it overflows to those around me.

184 I am a loving and kind partner in my relationships.

185 I choose love over fear and I am courageous in my actions.

186 I am worthy of being cherished, respected, and adored by my partner.

187 Love is a beautiful journey and I am excited to embark on it.

188 I am a loving and compassionate person towards myself and others.

189 I am grateful for the love that has shaped my life and I embrace it fully.

190 Love is my birthright and it is always available to me.

191 I am confident in my ability to create and nurture loving relationships.

192 I am surrounded by an abundance of love and positive energy.

193 I am lovable and capable of giving and receiving love.

194 I am loved beyond measure, and it fills me with happiness and joy.

195 Love gives me the strength and courage to face my fears.

196 I am grateful for the love I have experienced in the past, present, and future.

197 I am worthy of being loved and appreciated for who I am.

198 I am surrounded by love, kindness, and compassion.

199 Love brings me inner peace and contentment.

200 I am deserving of love and respect in all aspects of my life.

201 Love is a beautiful and powerful force that brings me happiness.

202 I am open to giving and receiving love in all its forms.

203 Love is an adventure, and I am excited for the journey.

204 I radiate love, kindness, and positivity, and it attracts more love into my life.

205 I am worthy of a love that is pure, true, and unconditional.

206 Love brings me joy, and I am grateful for all the love in my life.

207 I am surrounded by people who love and accept me just as I am.

208 I am deserving of a healthy, supportive, and fulfilling love life.

209 Love gives me the strength to overcome any obstacle.

210 I am grateful for the love that fills my heart and soul.

211 I am confident in my ability to attract and maintain loving relationships.

212 I am surrounded by love and it brings me peace and serenity.

213 I am worthy of being loved and appreciated by my partner.

214 Love is my true essence, and it fills me with joy and purpose.

215 I am deserving of a love that is honest, loyal, and faithful.

12. 217 Powerful Positive Affirmations For Abundance

1 I am abundant and deserving of wealth and success.

2 I am grateful for the abundance that flows into my life.

3 I am a magnet for prosperity and abundance.

4 Abundance comes naturally and effortlessly to me.

5 I am surrounded by abundance and opportunity.

6 I have an abundance mindset and I am open to receiving abundance in all forms.

7 I trust that the universe is abundant and that abundance is available to me.

8 I am open and receptive to all forms of abundance in my life.

9 I am worthy of receiving abundance and success.

10 I am grateful for the abundance that has come into my life and for what is yet to come.

11 I am capable of achieving my financial goals and creating the life I desire.

12 I am surrounded by positive and abundant energy that supports my goals.

13 I am confident in my ability to attract abundance and prosperity.

14 Abundance is my natural state of being.

15 I am grateful for the abundance that I already have in my life.

16 I am capable of creating wealth and financial success.

17 I am deserving of abundance and prosperity in all areas of my life.

18 I am open and receptive to the abundance that flows into my life.

19 I am worthy of living an abundant life filled with success and prosperity.

20 I am confident in my ability to manifest abundance and create the life I desire.

21 Abundance is available to me in all areas of my life.

22 I am grateful for the abundance that is already present in my life.

23 I am deserving of abundance and prosperity, and I embrace it fully.

24 I am surrounded by positive and supportive people who encourage my success.

25 Abundance is my birthright, and I claim it with gratitude and joy.

26 I am grateful for the abundance that is already present in my life, and I celebrate it.

27 I am worthy of abundance, prosperity, and success, and I claim it.

28 I am capable of creating wealth and financial success in my life.

29 I am deserving of an abundant life, and I embrace it fully.

30 I am confident in my ability to attract abundance and create the life I desire.

31 I am surrounded by supportive people who encourage my success and abundance.

32 Abundance is my natural state of being, and I accept it with gratitude and joy.

33 I am worthy of abundance and success in all areas of my life.

34 I am deserving of abundance, prosperity, and success, and I claim it.

35 Abundance is my birthright, and I embrace it with joy and gratitude.

36 I am worthy of abundance and prosperity, and I claim it fully.

37 I am capable of achieving all of my financial goals with ease and grace.

38 I am surrounded by opportunities for abundance and prosperity.

39 I am open and receptive to all the abundance that flows into my life.

Positive Affirmations For Black Men

40 I am deserving of abundance and success, and I accept it with open arms.

41 I am confident in my ability to create a life of abundance and prosperity.

42 Abundance is a natural and effortless state of being for me.

43 I am worthy of abundance and prosperity, and I claim it with gratitude and joy.

44 I am capable of creating and maintaining financial success and abundance.

45 I am surrounded by positive energy that supports my abundance and prosperity.

46 I am open and receptive to all the opportunities for abundance that come my way.

47 I am deserving of abundance and success, and I embrace it fully.

48 I am surrounded by supportive people who encourage my abundance and prosperity.

49 Abundance is my natural state of being, and I claim it with confidence and joy.

50 I am surrounded by opportunities for abundance and success.

51 I am deserving of abundance and success, and I embrace it with joy and gratitude.

52 I am capable of achieving all of my financial goals and creating the life I desire.

53 Abundance is my natural state of being, and I accept it with joy and gratitude.

54 I am worthy of abundance and prosperity, and I claim it with confidence and joy.

55 I am capable of creating a life of abundance and success in all areas of my life.

56 I am confident in my ability to create wealth and financial success in my life.

57 I am open and receptive to all the abundance and opportunities that come my way.

58 I am confident in my ability to create a life of abundance and prosperity, and I claim it fully.

59 I am abundant and deserving of all the good things that come my way.

60 I feel grateful for the abundance that surrounds me and flows into my life.

61 Abundance comes naturally and effortlessly to me, and I welcome it with joy and excitement.

62 I feel empowered and confident in my ability to attract abundance and prosperity into my life.

63 I am surrounded by abundance and opportunities that excite me and inspire me to take action.

64 I feel open and receptive to all the abundance and blessings that the universe has to offer.

65 I am grateful for the abundance that is already present in my life, and I trust that more is on the way.

66 I feel worthy of receiving abundance and success, and I claim it with confidence and excitement.

67 I am capable of creating a life of abundance and prosperity, and I am excited to see what the future holds.

68 I am surrounded by positive and supportive energy that uplifts me and motivates me to achieve my goals.

69 I feel abundant and prosperous in all areas of my life, and I embrace it with gratitude and joy.

70 I feel confident and empowered to take action and create the life of abundance that I desire.

71 I am open and receptive to all forms of abundance, and I trust that I am deserving of all the good things that come my way.

72 I feel inspired and motivated to attract abundance and prosperity into my life, and I am excited to see my dreams manifest.

73 I am grateful for the abundance that is already present in my life, and I look forward to experiencing even more abundance and blessings.

74 I feel worthy of abundance and success, and I trust that I am on the path to achieving all of my financial goals and aspirations.

75 I am surrounded by abundance and opportunities that inspire me to dream big and take action.

76 I feel confident and capable of creating a life of abundance and prosperity that aligns with my highest values and aspirations.

Positive Affirmations For Black Men

77 I am open and receptive to all the abundance and blessings that are available to me, and I trust that I am on the path to achieving all of my dreams and goals.

78 I feel grateful for the abundance and prosperity that is already present in my life, and I look forward to experiencing even more abundance and blessings in the future.

79 I feel empowered and confident in my ability to attract abundance and success into my life, and I trust that I am deserving of all the good things that come my way.

80 I am surrounded by positive and supportive energy that motivates me to take action and create the life of abundance that I desire.

81 I feel abundant and prosperous in all areas of my life, and I am excited to see what the future holds.

82 I am open and receptive to all the abundance and opportunities that come my way, and I trust that I am on the path to achieving all of my financial goals and aspirations.

83 I feel confident and capable of creating a life of abundance and prosperity that brings me joy and fulfillment.

84 I am surrounded by abundance and opportunities that inspire me to dream big and take action towards my goals.

85 I feel grateful for the abundance and prosperity that is already present in my life, and I trust that more is on the way.

86 I am open and receptive to all the abundance and opportunities that come my way, and I trust that the universe is conspiring in my favor.

87 I feel excited and motivated to take action towards creating the life of abundance and prosperity that I desire.

88 I am capable of manifesting all the abundance and prosperity that I desire, and I am excited to see my dreams come to fruition.

89 I feel grateful for the abundance that is already present in my life, and I am excited to see more abundance and blessings flow into my life.

90 I am worthy of all the good things that come my way, and I trust that abundance and prosperity are always available to me.

91 I am surrounded by abundance and opportunities that align with my highest values and aspirations.

92 I feel confident and empowered to take action towards creating the life of abundance and prosperity that I desire.

93 I am open and receptive to all the abundance and blessings that the universe has to offer, and I trust that I am deserving of all the good things that come my way.

94 I am grateful for the abundance and prosperity that is already present in my life, and I trust that more is on the way.

95 I feel excited and motivated to take action towards achieving all of my financial goals and aspirations.

96 I am surrounded by positive and supportive energy that uplifts me and motivates me to achieve my dreams.

97 I am confident in my ability to create a life of abundance and prosperity that aligns with my highest values and aspirations.

98 I am open and receptive to all the abundance and opportunities that come my way, and I trust that I am on the path to achieving all of my financial goals.

99 I feel worthy of abundance and success, and I trust that I am deserving of all the good things that come my way.

100 I am surrounded by abundance and opportunities that inspire me to take action and create the life of abundance that I desire.

101 I feel confident and empowered to take action towards achieving all of my financial goals and aspirations, and I am excited to see what the future holds.

102 I feel abundant and prosperous in all areas of my life, and I trust that more abundance and prosperity are on the way.

103 I am capable of creating a life of abundance and prosperity that aligns with my highest values and aspirations, and I am excited to take action towards achieving my goals.

104 I feel confident and empowered to take action towards achieving all of my financial goals and aspirations, and I am excited to see my dreams come to fruition.

105 I am worthy of all the abundance and prosperity that comes my way, and I trust that the universe always supports me in achieving my goals.

106 I am grateful for the abundance that is already present in my life, and I am excited to see more abundance and blessings flow into my life.

Positive Affirmations For Black Men

107 I feel confident and empowered to take action towards creating the life of abundance and prosperity that aligns with my highest values and aspirations.

108 I am capable of achieving all of my financial goals and aspirations, and I am excited to take action towards making my dreams a reality.

109 I am capable of creating a life of abundance and prosperity that brings me joy and fulfillment, and I am excited to take action towards making my dreams a reality.

110 I am open and receptive to all the abundance and blessings that the universe has to offer, and I trust that more abundance and prosperity are on the way.

111 I feel grateful for the abundance and prosperity that is already present in my life, and I am excited to see more abundance and blessings flow into my life.

112 I am open and receptive to all the abundance and opportunities that come my way, and I trust that the universe is always working in my favor.

113 I am surrounded by positive and supportive people who believe in my dreams and uplift me as I work towards achieving my goals.

114 I feel grateful for the abundance and prosperity that is already present in my life, and I trust that more is on the way. I am open and receptive to all the abundance and blessings that the universe has to offer, and I trust that I am deserving of all the good things that come my way. I feel confident and empowered to take action towards creating a life of abundance and prosperity that brings me joy and fulfillment.

115 I believe in my ability to create abundance in my life, and I trust that the universe is always working in my favor.

116 I am surrounded by opportunities for abundance and prosperity, and I am excited to take action towards achieving my goals.

117 I feel worthy of all the good things that come my way, and I trust that abundance and prosperity are always available to me.

118 I feel confident and empowered to take action towards achieving all of my financial goals and aspirations.

119 I feel excited and motivated to take action towards creating a life of abundance and prosperity that brings me joy and fulfillment.

120 I trust that the universe has a plan for me and that I am on the path to receiving all the abundance and prosperity that I desire.

121 I trust that my hard work and dedication will pay off, and I am excited to see the abundance and prosperity that will flow into my life as a result.

122 I trust that I am on the path to achieving all of my financial goals, and I am excited to see what the future holds.

123 I am capable of creating a life of abundance and prosperity that is aligned with my values and purpose, and I am excited to take action towards making my dreams a reality.

124 I am surrounded by abundance and prosperity that inspires me to take action and create the life that I desire.

125 I am surrounded by positive and supportive people who uplift me and inspire me to achieve my goals.

126 I am open and receptive to all the abundance and prosperity that comes my way, and I trust that the universe is always working in my favor.

127 I trust that I am on the path to receiving all the abundance and prosperity that I desire, and I am excited to take action towards making my dreams a reality.

128 I am surrounded by abundance and opportunities that align with my values and purpose, and I am excited to take action towards creating the life that I desire.

129 I trust that the universe is always working in my favor, and I am excited to see the abundance and prosperity that will flow into my life as a result.

130 I am open and receptive to all the abundance and blessings that come my way, and I trust that I am deserving of all the good things that come my way.

131 I am worthy of abundance in all areas of my life, and I trust that the universe is always working in my favor.

132 I am open and receptive to all the abundance and blessings that come my way, and I am excited to see what the future holds.

133 I trust that my positive thoughts and actions will attract abundance and prosperity into my life.

134 I am surrounded by abundance and opportunities that align with my goals and passions.

135 I trust that abundance and prosperity are always available to me, and I am excited to see what the future holds.

136 I am open and receptive to all the abundance and prosperity that is available to me, and I trust that the universe is always working in my favor.

137 I trust that I am on the path to achieving all of my financial goals and aspirations, and I am excited to see what the future holds.

138 I feel confident and empowered to take action towards creating a life of abundance and prosperity that aligns with my highest values and aspirations.

139 I am capable of creating a life of abundance and prosperity that is aligned with my purpose and passions, and I am excited to take action towards making my dreams a reality.

140 I am worthy of all the abundance and prosperity that comes my way, and I trust that more is on the way.

141 I am surrounded by abundance and opportunities that inspire me to take action towards achieving my financial goals and aspirations.

142 I am confident in my ability to attract and manifest abundance and prosperity into my life.

143 I am deserving of financial abundance and prosperity, and I trust that the universe is always working in my favor.

144 I am open and receptive to new opportunities that will bring more abundance and prosperity into my life.

145 I am capable of creating a life of abundance and prosperity that allows me to live my best life and help others.

146 I am surrounded by abundance and prosperity that motivates me to take action towards achieving my financial goals and aspirations.

147 I am open and receptive to all the abundance and prosperity that the universe has in store for me.

148 I am worthy of abundance and prosperity, and I am confident in my ability to attract and manifest it into my life.

149 I trust that all of my financial needs and desires will be met, and I am excited to see how abundance and prosperity will flow into my life.

150 I am surrounded by positive and supportive people who believe in me and my ability to create a life of abundance and prosperity.

151 I am capable of creating a life of abundance and prosperity that allows me to live my best life and positively impact the world.

152 I am open and receptive to all the abundance and blessings that the universe has in store for me, and I trust that I am deserving of all the good things that come

my way.

153 I am surrounded by abundance and prosperity that inspires me to take action towards achieving my financial goals and aspirations.

154 I am grateful for the abundance and prosperity that is already present in my life, and I am excited to see how more abundance and prosperity will flow into my life.

155 I am confident in my ability to attract and manifest abundance and prosperity into my life, and I am excited to see what the future holds.

156 I trust that abundance and prosperity are always available to me, and I am open and receptive to all the blessings that come my way.

157 I am capable of creating a life of abundance and prosperity that allows me to live my best life and fulfill my highest purpose.

158 I am surrounded by abundance and opportunities that motivate me to take action towards achieving my financial goals and aspirations.

159 I am worthy of all the abundance and prosperity that comes my way, and I am grateful for all the good things that are already present in my life.

160 I am open and receptive to all the abundance and blessings that the universe has in store for me, and I trust that more is on the way.

161 I trust that I am on the path to achieving all of my financial goals and aspirations, and I am excited to see how abundance and prosperity will flow into my life.

162 I am capable of creating a life of abundance and prosperity that aligns with my values and purpose, and I am excited to take action towards making my dreams a reality.

163 I am surrounded by abundance and prosperity that aligns with my highest values and aspirations, and I am excited to take action towards achieving my financial goals.

164 I am confident in my ability to attract abundance and prosperity into my life, and I am open and receptive to all the opportunities that come my way.

165 I am deserving of abundance and prosperity, and I am excited to take action towards creating a life of financial freedom and abundance.

166 I am surrounded by abundance and prosperity that motivates me to take inspired action towards achieving my goals and aspirations.

Positive Affirmations For Black Men

167 I am capable of creating a life of abundance and prosperity that allows me to live my best life and make a positive impact on the world.

168 I am open and receptive to all the abundance and blessings that the universe has in store for me, and I am excited to see what the future holds.

169 I am surrounded by abundance and prosperity that aligns with my values and purpose, and I am excited to take action towards achieving my financial goals and aspirations.

170 I am confident in my ability to attract and manifest abundance and prosperity into my life, and I am excited to see how abundance and prosperity will flow into my life.

171 I am surrounded by abundance and opportunities that align with my values and passions, and I am excited to take action towards achieving my financial goals and aspirations.

172 I am worthy of all the abundance and prosperity that comes my way, and I am excited to take action towards creating a life of financial freedom and abundance.

173 Abundance flows to me effortlessly and joyfully.

174 I am a magnet for abundance and prosperity.

175 I am grateful for the abundance that surrounds me.

176 I trust that abundance is my natural state of being.

177 I deserve to have abundance in all areas of my life.

178 I am worthy of receiving abundance and prosperity.

179 I am open and receptive to all the abundance and blessings that come my way.

180 I feel abundance and prosperity in every aspect of my life.

181 I am excited to see how abundance and prosperity will continue to flow into my life.

182 I am surrounded by abundance and prosperity that inspires me to take action towards my goals.

183 Abundance is a feeling that I cultivate within myself every day.

184 I am open to all the opportunities that come my way, and I trust that they will lead to abundance and prosperity.

185 I trust that the universe is always working in my favor, and abundance is on its way to me.

186 I feel abundant and prosperous in all areas of my life.

187 I am worthy of the abundance and prosperity that flows into my life.

188 I am grateful for the abundance and prosperity that is already present in my life, and I am excited to see how more will flow in.

189 I am capable of creating a life of abundance and prosperity that aligns with my values and purpose.

190 I am surrounded by abundance and prosperity that brings me joy and happiness.

191 Abundance is my birthright, and I claim it now.

192 I am open and receptive to all the abundance and blessings that the universe has in store for me.

193 I feel abundant and prosperous every day, and I am grateful for all the good things in my life.

194 I trust that the universe is always providing for me, and I am open to receiving all the abundance and prosperity that comes my way.

195 I am surrounded by abundance and prosperity that motivates me to take action towards my goals and aspirations.

196 I am worthy of all the abundance and prosperity that comes my way, and I am excited to see how more will flow into my life.

197 I am confident in my ability to attract and manifest abundance and prosperity into my life, and I am excited to see how it will manifest.

198 I trust that the universe is always working in my favor, and I am open and receptive to all the abundance and prosperity that comes my way.

199 I am capable of creating a life of abundance and prosperity that allows me to live my best life and positively impact others.

200 I am surrounded by abundance and prosperity that aligns with my values and purpose, and I am excited to take action towards achieving my financial goals.

201 I feel abundant and prosperous in all areas of my life, and I am grateful for all the good things that come my way.

Positive Affirmations For Black Men

202 I am worthy of abundance and prosperity, and I trust that the universe is always providing for me.

203 I am open and receptive to all the abundance and blessings that come my way, and I am excited to see how it will continue to flow into my life.

204 I am confident in my ability to create a life of abundance and prosperity that allows me to live my best life and positively impact the world.

205 I am surrounded by abundance and prosperity that motivates me to take inspired action towards my goals and aspirations.

206 I am grateful for the abundance and prosperity that is already present in my life, and I trust that more is on its way.

207 I am surrounded by abundance and prosperity that inspires me to pursue my passions and follow my dreams.

208 I feel a sense of abundance and prosperity in all areas of my life, and I am excited to see how it will continue to grow.

209 I am confident in my ability to attract abundance and prosperity into my life, and I am open to receiving it in all forms.

210 I am open and receptive to all the opportunities that come my way, and I am excited to see how they will lead to abundance and prosperity.

211 I trust that abundance and prosperity are my birthright, and I am excited to claim it.

212 I am capable of creating a life of abundance and prosperity that aligns with my values and brings me joy and happiness.

213 I am surrounded by abundance and prosperity that motivates me to take action towards achieving my goals and aspirations.

214 I am grateful for all the abundance and prosperity that is present in my life, and I am excited to see how more will flow in.

215 I trust that the universe is always working in my favor, and I am excited to see how abundance and prosperity will continue to flow into my life.

216 I am surrounded by abundance and prosperity that inspires me to take action towards my financial goals and aspirations.

217 I feel a sense of abundance and prosperity in all areas of my life, and I am grateful for all the good things that come my way.

Conclusion

As you come to the end of this book, "Positive Affirmations For Black Men," you have taken the first step towards a journey of transformation. Your mind has been rewired with positive affirmations that have equipped you with the tools needed to achieve success in all areas of your life.

Remember that success is not a destination, but a journey. It is a journey that requires hard work, dedication, and a positive mindset. Use the affirmations in this book to guide you on this journey and to help you overcome any challenges that may arise.

You are capable of achieving greatness, and with the power of positive affirmations, you can manifest your dreams and desires into reality. Believe in yourself, trust in your abilities, and continue to speak positivity into your life.

As you move forward on this journey, always remember to keep a positive attitude, and don't be afraid to ask for help when you need it. The universe is conspiring in your favor, and with a positive mindset and the right mindset, you will attract all the wealth, health, confidence, and abundance you desire.

So go ahead and start your 30-day journey of positive affirmations, and watch as your life transforms in ways you never thought possible. Remember, you are destined for greatness, and the power to achieve it lies within you!

Reference List & Resources

100 Affirmations For Self Love & Unshakable Confidence — The Spirit Nomad. (2021). Retrieved 11 March 2021, from https://www.thespiritnomad.com/blog/affirmations/

100 Positive Affirmations for Success and How to Use Them - Completed Thoughts. Retrieved 5 March 2021, from https://completedthoughts.com/positive-affirmations-for-success/

100 Self Love Affirmations to Build your Self Esteem. Retrieved 8 March 2021, from https://www.throughthephases.com/self-love-affirmations/

101 Exercise & Fitness Affirmations For Working Out. Retrieved 14 March 2021, from https://motivationping.com/exercise-fitness-affirmations-quotes/

218 Affirmations For Protection And Grounding - The Right Affirmations. The Right Affirmations. Retrieved 19 September 2021, from https://therightaffirmations.com/affirmations-for-protection/.

30 Positive Sleep Affirmations to Relax at Night! | PRANCIER. PRANCIER. (2021). Retrieved 19 September 2021, from https://prancier.com/blog/positive-sleep-affirmations.

50 Powerful Financial Affirmations for Manifesting Money!. (2021). Retrieved 5 March 2021, from https://stackyourdollars.com/financial-affirmations-manifesting-money/

55 Positive Sleep Affirmations for a Restful Night. Healthy Happy Impactful. (2020). Retrieved 19 September 2021, from https://healthyhappyimpactful.com/night-sleep-affirmations/.

643 Affirmations For Financial Freedom, Wealth, Abundance, Money and Prosperity | Yes Financially Free. (2015). Retrieved 12 March 2021, from https://yesfinanciallyfree.com/643-affirmations-for-financial-freedom-wealth-abundance-money-and-prosperity/

75 Success Affirmations That Will Boost Your Confidence. Retrieved 11 March 2021, from https://motivationping.com/success-affirmations/

79 Powerful Affirmations for Money That Will Help You Improve Your Financial Situation. (2020). Retrieved 2 March 2021, from https://thriveglobal.com/stories/79-powerful-affirmations-for-money-that-will-help-you-improve-your-financial-situation/

AVILA, T. (2019). 20 Money Mantras To Inspire Financial Freedom - Girlboss. Retrieved 15 March 2021, from https://www.girlboss.com/read/money-mantras-affirmations

BOLDER, A. (2020). 30 POWERFUL AFFIRMATIONS FOR ENTREPRENEURS AND BUSINESS SUCCESS | AndreaBolder.com | Biz Tips For Female Entrepreneurs. Retrieved 5 March 2021, from https://andreabolder.com/affirmations-business-success/

Brennan, T. (2021). 21 positive sleep affirmations for a good night's rest. Vertellis. Retrieved 19 September 2021, from https://vertellis.com/blogs/all/sleep-affirmations.

Brock, F. 25 Money Affirmations to Attract Wealth and Abundance | Prolific Living. Retrieved 11 March 2021, from https://www.prolificliving.com/money-affirmations/

Camp, N. (2016). 100 Success Affirmations For All Areas of Your Life. Retrieved 12 March 2021, from https://committedtomyself.com/100-success-affirmations-for-all-areas-of-your-life/

Confidence Affirmations For Believing In Yourself. (2021). Retrieved 11 March 2021, from https://motivationping.com/confidence-affirmations/

DANIELS, E. (2021). 50 Positive Quotes and Messages To Improve Someone's Day - Shari's Berries Blog. Shari's Berries Blog. Retrieved 10 February 2021, from https://www.berries.com/blog/positive-quotes.

Davis, R. (2013). 66 Health, Fitness, and Weight Loss Affirmations. Retrieved 17 March 2021, from https://affirmationspot.me/2012/01/09/41-health-fitness-and-weight-loss-affirmations/

Reference List & Resources

Derosa, D. (2017). 50 Self-Loving Affirmations – Uncover Your Joy | Healing from Abuse. Retrieved 13 March 2021, from https://uncoveryourjoy.com/50-self-loving-affirmations/

Dowches-Wheeler, J. (2018). 30 Affirmations for Confidence — Jessica DW | Find Your Purpose. Retrieved 16 March 2021, from https://jessicadw.com/blog/2018/4/13/30-affirmations-for-confidence

Dowches-Wheeler, J. (2020). 60 Abundance Affirmations to Transform Your Mindset — Jessica DW | Find Your Purpose. Retrieved 6 March 2021, from https://jessicadw.com/blog/60-abundance-affirmations-money-affirmations

Dulin, D. (2021). 100 Positive Thinking Quotes To Help You Achieve Greatness. Unfinished Success | Reach Your Full Potential. Retrieved 1 March 2021, from https://www.unfinishedsuccess.com/positive-thinking-quotes/.

Finn, A. (2021). 150 Positive Quotes and Positive Thinking Sayings. Quote Ambition. Retrieved 5 March 2021, from https://www.quoteambition.com/positive-thinking-quotes/.

Fitness Training Positive Affirmations – Free Affirmations – Free Positive Affirmations. Retrieved 13 March 2021, from https://www.freeaffirmations.org/fitness-training-positive-affirmations

Gaille, B. (2020). 100 Powerful Money Affirmations for Financial Abundance. Retrieved 11 March 2021, from https://brandongaille.com/money-affirmations/

Gaille, B. (2020). 100 Powerful Money Affirmations for Financial Abundance. Retrieved 17 March 2021, from https://brandongaille.com/money-affirmations/

Hurst, K. (2020). 50 Morning Affirmations For Success And Confidence. Retrieved 8 March 2021, from https://www.thelawofattraction.com/morning-affirmations-success/

Johnson, L. (2021). 25 Daily Positive Thinking Affirmations for Success | Lisa Johnson. Retrieved 17 March 2021, from https://lisajohnsoncoaching.co.uk/daily-positive-thinking-affirmation/#:~:text=Here's%2025%20daily%20positive%20thinking,I%20love%20myself.

Juma, N. (2021). 195 Positive Thinking Quotes For A New Perspective. Everyday Power. Retrieved 2 March 2021, from https://everydaypower.com/positive-thinking-quotes/.

Kyle, K. 100+ I Am Affirmations For Abundance: I Am A Money Magnet. Retrieved 11 March 2021, from https://www.kathkyle.com/i-am-affirmations-for-abundance/

Michalowicz, M. (2017). If You Believe, You Can Achieve - 40 Affirmations for Small Business Owners - Small Business Trends. Retrieved 11 March 2021, from https://smallbiztrends.com/2017/01/small-business-affirmations.html

Mishra, A. (2021). Become A Money Magnet: 55 Powerful Money Affirmations You Must Use. Retrieved 3 March 2021, from https://awesomeaj.com/2015/03/26/money-magnet-powerful-money-affirmations/

Mitchell, S. (2019). 71 AWESOME CONFIDENCE-BOOSTING AFFIRMATIONS TO SLAY YOUR EVERYDAY | In Her Worlds. Retrieved 11 March 2021, from https://inherworlds.com/confidence-boosting-affirmations/

Perez, D. (2019). 25 Health Affirmations for Your Healthiest Self!. Retrieved 15 March 2021, from https://wildsimplejoy.com/affirmations-for-health-fitness/

Sutherland, C. (2018). 10 Affirmations To Create Wealth. Retrieved 14 March 2021, from https://thriveglobal.com/stories/10-affirmations-to-create-wealth/

Tomlinson, W. (2021). 21+ empowering affirmations for business success | Morning Business Chat. Retrieved 1 March 2021, from https://morningbusinesschat.com/21-affirmations-business-success/

Top 100 Positive Quotes | 110 Quotes About Positivity In Life. Be An Inspirer. (2019). Retrieved 25 February 2021, from https://www.beaninspirer.com/top-100-positive-quotes/.

Williamson, J. (2018). 25 Loving Affirmations for Health That Respect the Healing Process. Retrieved 14 March 2021, from https://healingbrave.com/blogs/all/affirmations-for-health-healing-process

Reference List & Resources

Yalım, D. (2019). 90+ Best Quotes From Famous Actors and Actresses. Bayart.org. Retrieved 2 February 2021, from https://bayart.org/quotes-from-actors-actresses/.

Zhang, J. (2020). 101 I Am Affirmations for Success, Abundance, Wealth and Happiness. Retrieved 10 March 2021, from https://www.emoovio.com/i-am-affirmations/

Zhang, J. (2020). 110 Healing Affirmations for Body, Mind & Soul Repair. Retrieved 14 March 2021, from https://www.emoovio.com/healing-affirmations/

Printed in Great Britain
by Amazon